NIGHT
JOURNEY

NIGHT JOURNEY

A Story of Survival and Deliverance

John G. Stoessinger

A Playboy Press Book

FIRST EDITION

Playboy and Rabbit Head design are trademarks of Playboy, 919 North Michigan Avenue, Chicago, Illinois 66011 (U.S.A.), reg. U.S. Pat., marca registrada, marque déposée.

Trade distribution by Simon and Schuster
A Division of Gulf + Western Corporation
New York, New York 10020

Designed by Tere LoPrete

Library of Congress Cataloging in Publication Data

Stoessinger, John George.
    Night journey.

    1. Stoessinger, John George.   2. Political scientist
—United States—Biography.   I. Title.
JA93.S85A35   320'.092'4 [B]   78-15265
ISBN 0-87223-512-2

FOR
Anna Elizabeth

He who lives more lives than one
More deaths than one must die.

Oscar Wilde

NIGHT JOURNEY

PART I

Chapter One

School was closed. A holiday had been declared all over Austria. Tens of thousands of Viennese had dressed in their Sunday best and were straining toward the Ringstrasse. The mood was festive and church bells tolled incessantly. The city had turned out en masse to greet its new Führer. Everywhere, houses were adorned with spring flowers, and decked out with large swastika flags.

The Ringstrasse, the main thoroughfare of Vienna, was a great boulevard circling the entire city. It seemed that all of Vienna was lining "the Ring" to celebrate Austria's absorption into the Reich; it was the day of the Anschluss. Adolf Hitler was making his triumphal entry into Vienna in a grand motorcade several miles long. He was to be welcomed by the blaring of trumpets and the thunder of drums, by scores and scores of marching bands. Along with the bands marched the vast goose-stepping armies of the Wehrmacht, the SS and the SA. The German leader was to ride past the waving throngs of Viennese in an open limousine.

The crowd lining the Ringstrasse had already begun to cheer. Latecomers, fearful of missing the parade, were running in the same direction. Young couples, eyes laughing and arms intertwined, overtook the older folks. Thin, and only ten years old, I ran faster than most. I, too, was eager to get a glimpse of the German Führer who was coming to annex my hometown.

Lisl had promised that she would wait for me at the Beethoven statue near the Ring. She was a music student at the Vienna Academy of Art. My mother had hired her as a part-time governess and piano teacher for me.

Lisl was twenty-three, Catholic, and very beautiful. Her eyes were the color of cornflowers and her blond hair reached down almost to her waist. She had told me about Schubert's early death at thirty-one. Together we had pilgrimaged to Heiligenstadt, to pay homage to Beethoven; but her favorite was Mozart. Once she had taken me to St. Stephen's Cathedral to hear the great C Minor Mass.

"When the angels are on duty in heaven," Lisl had said, "they play Bach; but off duty, they play Mozart."

When she told me afterward that Mozart was buried in an unknown grave, she had wept. I had promised her that someday I would try to find Mozart's grave. I would have promised Lisl anything to stop her tears. I was in love with her.

I could not spot Lisl right away. By now, people were packed ten deep along the Ringstrasse, all eyes riveted on the steel-helmeted storm troopers on motorcycles who formed the vanguard of Hitler's victory procession. Soon a row of cars appeared and the shouting became louder. I pushed my way through the crowd, searching for Lisl.

"The Führer will pass here in five minutes," I heard a high-pitched voice exclaim behind me. At that moment I saw Lisl standing in the front row. Happily, I pushed through the last few feet of the cheering throng, and reached for Lisl's hand.

Lisl glanced down at me. I had never seen her look more beautiful. Yet she seemed strangely distant and did not give my hand that reassuring squeeze of recognition. I became uneasy.

"We must be silent," she whispered almost reverently. "The Führer's car is coming."

I nodded obediently, studying Lisl's face. Her deep blue eyes seemed to burn with an ardent fire and her hair was windblown in the March breeze. At that very moment a great roar went through the crowd. An open automobile had become visible in the distance. It was moving toward us very slowly. In it stood a solitary figure, his arm outstretched in a stiff salute. Lisl let go of my hand and reached for the little golden cross that she wore between her breasts. It was a gesture she made habitually when reciting the Lord's Prayer to me at bedtime. "It's a prayer Jews can say too," she liked to say on those occasions.

Hitler's car was inching closer and then, for some unknown reason, came to a complete standstill almost directly in front of us, only a few feet away. The cheering all around us had risen to a deafening crescendo: "We thank our Führer. We thank our Führer." Again and again the crowd chanted the same refrain. I still looked at Lisl clutching her cross. Her eyes had become glazed.

"Holy Maria, Mother of God," she whispered. "He is the new Messiah." I turned to look at the figure in the now stationary car. Hitler had dropped his arm for a moment and was smiling. It seemed to me that he was looking directly at Lisl. He seemed handsome and kind as he stood there smiling. With a pang of recognition I fixed my eyes on his mustache.

Just like Papa's, I thought. My beloved father, who used to tickle the soles of my feet with his mustache as he kissed them and who had disappeared years ago without a trace. I had been heartbroken when Papa vanished. I had looked for him for weeks. Convinced that it was my fault that he had gone away, I had promised Mama that I would never be bad again.

"Please make him come back," I pleaded. My mother only cried.

One day, I thought I saw him on the street and ran into an oncoming car. Luckily, the driver had braked just in time and I escaped with only a few bruises.

"For a big boy of five, you shouldn't be so careless," the doctor had warned me. Nevertheless, I thought I saw Papa everywhere. The pain was like a wild animal raging inside me. Gradually, its grip lessened, but never left entirely. Papa's sudden disappearance remained a mystery.

Hitler's car lurched forward. I was awakened from my reverie by Lisl's voice.

"He has the most beautiful eyes," she said worshipfully. "Did you notice?"

I hadn't noticed. I had been thinking about Papa.

"Will Hitler be my Führer too?" I asked.

Lisl's face became grave as she placed her hand gently on my head. "I don't think so," she replied. "Hitler does not want to be the Führer of the Jews." Then she took me home, through the Stadtpark and the festive crowd.

"Mama, you are part Aryan, aren't you?" I asked my mother hopefully during lunch. My mother had blond hair and blue eyes and fitted the description of the ideal Aryan that I had heard about in school.

"No, I am not," Mama answered. "I am Jewish and so are you."

"One hundred percent?" I asked. Mama nodded. "Well, I don't want to be Jewish any longer," I blurted out.

The day before I had been beaten up by some of my classmates who, only a few weeks earlier, had made it a daily practice to copy my homework. Now all the boys in school, except for a handful of Jews, were Hitler Youth, and everything had changed. Even the clothes. The *Hitlerjugend*

proudly wore their new uniforms with the swastika armbands, the shining belt buckles, and the glittering daggers
that bore the inscription "Alles für Deutschland." I was
tired of being an outsider and the only Jew in the class.
"Why does Hitler say that everything is the fault of the
Jews?" I asked my mother.

"Yes, the Jews and the bicyclists," Mama answered.

"Why the bicyclists?" I asked, surprised.

"Why the Jews?" retorted my mother, with a small sad
smile.

I looked at her and then at Lisl, waiting for an explanation.
None was offered. I was confused. Mama seemed lost in
thought. Lisl looked at her and then at me. But she did not
smile.

"Come, let's go for a walk," Mama said to me as she rose
from the table.

My mother was a beautiful woman who was proud of her
resemblance to Marlene Dietrich. She was out much of the
time and I was left in Lisl's care and that of Emma,
the elderly cook.

"Where have you been?" I would ask my mother when
she returned in the evenings.

"Shopping," Mama would say with an easy laugh, pulling me toward her. She would shower me with kisses and
endearments, but after a few minutes she would become
impatient. "Emma!" she called out into the kitchen. "Is dinner ready?"

After dinner, Mama would usually go out for the evening, but sometimes she sat down at the piano and sang the
latest Viennese hits. Once in a while, she would take me to
a concert or a play at the Burgtheater. I cherished those brief
moments in the company of my mother. Men, I noticed,
would kiss her hand and look at her with admiration.

"Meet my little prince," she would say, and a strange
man's hand would pat my head perfunctorily.

Sometimes she would be gone for days at a time. I never found out what Mama bought on those shopping trips since she rarely brought anything home. All I knew was that I hated them. I would sulk in my room and Lisl and Emma would do their best to comfort me. I knew that Mama usually returned at dinner time and I would listen for her footsteps.

"How's the little prince?" she would ask as Emma opened the door.

"He's been waiting for you," answered the cook in a tone of mild reproach. "I just fixed his favorite dessert."

"I'll have some too," said my mother, "but let's eat quickly, I am going out again at eight o'clock."

During dinner mother would ask me questions about my homework. They were always easy. "My clever little prince," she would say proudly, with a laugh, "you'll be a king yet, or at least a prime minister."

Now, as we walked through the Stadtpark, Mama was serious. Swastika flags fluttered everywhere—from the park's trees, its fountains and war memorials, and its statues of generals, artists, and composers. Someone had even stuck one into the hand of the Schubert statue. The composer's cherubic face looked impassively into the distance. Incongruously, a pigeon had settled on Schubert's head, and relieved itself.

"That's how Vienna treats its geniuses," my mother said sadly.

I thought of the *Unfinished Symphony*, which I had heard for the first time a month before. Its insistent yearning had stirred me deeply. That night I had dreamed of Papa again. The dream was always the same. I followed him into dark tunnels and alleys, but just when I thought I could touch him, he would recede into the distance. In the end, he always eluded me. When I awoke, I would lie in bed for hours, trying to recapture the image of his face. It had been so clear in the dream. But with the morning light, the image faded. Only the longing remained.

We emerged on the north side of the Stadtpark. The streets had become narrow and were paved with cobblestones. Mama had been silent for a while. Suddenly, with an effort, she turned to me and said, "We must leave Vienna. I am taking the train for Prague tonight. Opi and Omi want us to live there and have found us an apartment. I will come back next week and take you to Prague. In the meantime, Lisl will take care of you."

I nodded happily. An Austrian *Gymnasium* was a difficult place under any circumstances, but with the takeover by the Hitler Youth, the harassment and daily beatings, school had become a nightmare. Any chance to get away was welcome. Moreover, the prospect of a ride on the Vienna-Prague Express exhilarated me. Prague was an exciting city and I loved my grandparents whom I visited there every summer.

"How long will we stay in Prague?" I wanted to know.

Mama did not answer.

"Will Lisl come along?"

"No," my mother said. A sense of foreboding rose within me. I began to understand that this train ride to Prague would not be a routine vacation trip.

"Let's get an eclair," said Mama. Mama and I sometimes wandered around Vienna on Sundays. She would make it a habit to take me to her favorite pastry shop on the north side of the city, famous for its cream puffs and thick hot chocolate. But this was not Sunday. My foreboding deepened but I was too frightened to ask any more questions.

We trudged up the hilly Berggasse in silence. The sun had broken through the clouds. It was a beautiful afternoon with a hint of early spring. Halfway up the hill, my mother broke the silence with a small gasp.

"My God, I think here comes the dream doctor," she said.

I looked up. A very old man with a beard was coming toward us. He walked with short steps and held on to the arm of a younger woman.

"He will leave Vienna, too, the dream doctor," said Mama.

"Does he know what dreams mean?" I asked, fascinated.

"He has written a book about them," said Mama. "I tried to read it once but it made no sense at all to me. He is a famous old eccentric. His name is Dr. Sigmund Freud."

"What a beautiful name!" I exclaimed.

In school, we had sung Beethoven's chorale from the Ninth Symphony, set to Schiller's poem *An die Freude*. The words had made a deep impression on me.

"Can Dr. Freud make dreams have happy endings?" I wanted to know. I was thinking of my recurrent nightmare about Papa which always ended in the same frustration.

Mama broke into a cascade of affectionate laughter. "Maybe you should ask him yourself," she said.

We turned around. But the dream doctor and his companion were already at the bottom of the hill, well out of earshot.

Mama's mood had darkened again. Something about our encounter with Dr. Freud seemed to have upset her. Our visit to the pastry shop proved to be an anticlimax. We returned home by midafternoon. Lisl had already packed Mama's bags.

"Be a good boy," Mama said as she hugged me goodbye. "I will come back for you next week."

And she was gone.

I loved my piano lessons with Lisl. We would sit side by side on the piano bench and play Mozart sonatinas for four hands. Lisl would usually let me play the easier part with the melody. The scent of her perfume, next to me, would complete the enchantment. Once, quite by accident, my elbow touched her breast and an overpowering delicious sensation coursed through my entire body. After this incident, which went quite unnoticed by Lisl, I was unable to concentrate. So Lisl sat down alone at the piano and sang Schubert Lieder. She accompanied her rich alto voice with considerable skill. After that evening, I worshiped Lisl, and would practice endless hours to try to please her.

Tonight I looked forward to an evening alone with Lisl. It would make up for the sudden shock of Mama's announcement that we would leave Vienna soon. But during dinner Lisl seemed preoccupied, and when I asked her to play for me, she shook her head and announced that she had to go out to keep an appointment with a friend. Besides, she admonished, it would do me no harm if I practiced some Czerny exercises. Fearful of arousing Lisl's displeasure, I sat down at the piano. Lisl said that she would return in time to say goodnight. Then she left the house.

The stillness in the empty apartment was oppressive. The ticking of the old grandfather clock on the mantelpiece seemed unusually loud. I practiced for an hour and then gave up in disgust. My fingers were not obeying me. I was badly frightened and did not quite know why. My anxiety became so great that I went to my room, crawled into bed, and pulled the covers over my head. There I fell into a fitful sleep.

I awoke with a start. I had heard voices whispering in Mama's bedroom. Her room was next to mine, separated from it by a thick and heavy velvet curtain. The curtain had been installed the year before when I had come down with scarlet fever, and Mama would come in during the night and cool my burning forehead with ice cold compresses. Now my first thought was of burglars and I began to choke with fear. But then I recognized Lisl's voice, speaking in hushed whispers, laughing softly. Strange, I thought, only partially reassured. I knew that Lisl's little room was on the other side of mine. All was silent there.

For a while I lay in bed and listened to the whispers on the other side of the curtain. I thought I heard a man's voice too, but I could not quite hear what they were saying. I thought that I heard Lisl say, "It's all right, he's asleep." The whispering stopped and soon gave way to soft rhythmic moans that aroused my curiosity. Noiselessly, I slipped out of bed and crept toward the curtain. Getting up on tiptoe, I knew that I could look into my mother's bedroom by parting the curtain in the upper-left corner. I stretched my body to look and froze in horror.

There, on Mama's big and comfortable bed, lay Lisl and a large strange man, both completely naked. Lisl's face was visible in the dim moonlight and seemed distorted with pain. But she clutched the man to her body with both her arms.

Suddenly, a fierce whisper escaped Lisl's throat: "I want a son for the Führer!" The man groaned.

As in a trance, my eyes were riveted on the dark triangle below Lisl's belly. Her breasts were glistening with sweat and the little golden cross shimmered in the moonlight. Then I noticed that the man's clothes were strewn all over the bedroom floor.

I recognized the black uniform of the SS. A swastika armband and a belt with a silver buckle were visible on the chair. A pair of black boots and a holstered revolver were lying on the carpet.

My gaze returned to Lisl. She was smiling at the inert form next to her. "Stay a while," she whispered softly. The man sighed. Lisl lifted her face and whispered hoarsely: "Give me a son for the Führer." She reached for the cross between her breasts, clutched it with both hands, as if in prayer, and whispered reverently: "The new Messiah."

The man turned toward Lisl and reached for her. Suddenly, a terrible pain flooded my body. It was as if my guts were hungry wolves that were devouring me from within. My throat constricted. Almost unable to breathe, I staggered back to my bed and curled up. As the rhythmic moaning began again, the pain howled inside me. I stuffed the bedsheets into my mouth to stifle my sobs. I lay there, twisted with terror, long after I heard the SS officer leave Mama's room.

By next morning I had developed a raging fever. Lisl called the doctor who prescribed alternate hot and cold baths. My mother returned from Prague and sat by my bedside for three days and nights. I recovered slowly. My mother told me that the doctors had been unable to agree on a diagnosis, but that they had said that it was serious. I kept silent.

The following week we left for Prague. Lisl came to the station to say goodbye. She kissed me on the cheek. I felt nothing. Exhausted, I leaned back in a corner of the compartment. Vaguely, I thought of Papa and Dr. Freud, the dream doctor. A whistle blew and the train began to move. Mama cried. I couldn't. I never saw Lisl again.

Chapter Two

I leaned out of our third-story window in St. Wenceslaus Square, a great rectangular area in the center of Prague. Mama had forbidden me to leave the house. The atmosphere in the city was explosive. Hundreds of German tanks were said to be on the outskirts. Thousands of angry Czechs mobbed the square. A man near our window who shouted, "Shoot the traitors Chamberlain and Daladier," was applauded wildly by those nearby. Czech policemen in dark blue uniforms were cordoning off the crowd from the main thoroughfare, which had been cleared for the tanks.

Dusk was setting in and it was beginning to snow. Suddenly, I heard singing. Down below, someone had begun to sing the Czech national anthem. Soon, the entire crowd had joined in. Like a great mournful wave, the strains of the old hymn rolled across the square in the gathering dusk. "Where is my home? Where is my home?" It was the defiant farewell of a betrayed and conquered nation.

The policemen had locked arms and formed a human chain of blue uniforms to hold back the crowd. They, too, were singing. Some were weeping openly. The Czech policemen usually seemed so tall in their resplendent uniforms with the brass buttons; now I felt sorry for them. They looked like pallbearers at a funeral. Prague's last day of freedom was coming to an end.

I had come to love the Czech capital. My grandparents owned a shoe store near the square which they had built up over thirty years of hard work. Once a year, they took a week's vacation at an inexpensive nearby spa. One night, they ventured into the local casino to try roulette. They had invented a system so that they couldn't lose. Whenever grandfather bet red, grandmother would quickly place a matching bet on black. By ten o'clock, she had won ten crowns from grandfather. The house got nothing.

I would wait on customers in the shoe store after school hours. I had learned the language and made new friends, and I believed that I had left the Hitler Youth behind me for good. On weekends, we would drive into the surrounding woods. There, in the green silence, I would gather basketsful of blueberries. Unfailingly, grandmother rewarded me for my efforts with a silver five-crown piece. Then she would serve a tasty evening meal capped by those same blueberries that still bore the aroma of the Bohemian woods.

My grandfather was the kindest of men. He had taught me chess and even let me win occasionally. He also had a keen sense of humor. Once, a customer told an interminable story without a point and then, realizing that the punch line was missing, mumbled apologetically, "Goodness, now I have forgotten what I wanted to say."

"Never mind," grandfather said, shaking with laughter, "say something similar."

Even though pets made him nervous, he had bought me a little dog. I was his only grandchild.

Even school was not unpleasant. The teachers were gentle and had imagination. Our history teacher, for example, liked to refer to Hitler as Louis the Thirtieth.

"Why?" one of us inevitably asked.

"Because Louis the Fifteenth was a half-wit," Dr. Svoboda replied. We looked at him blankly. "That makes Hitler a total idiot," Dr. Svoboda explained.

Our teacher had also invented a game entitled "The Professor and the Idiot" which was very educational. It was to be played by two pupils, one assuming the role of history professor, the other that of idiot. The professor was to ask the idiot a question so simple that even a child would be able to answer it. It was then the idiot's task to give the wrong answer nonetheless, whereupon the professor had to "prove" that even the most stupid reply was in fact correct. Example: "How long was the Thirty Years' War?" Answer: "Seven years." Professor: "Correct, in those days, people did not fight at night, therefore one half of the actual fighting time may be subtracted. In addition, there was no fighting on weekends and holidays. If one further subtracts the numerous interruptions due to truces and peace negotiations, one arrives at a precise fighting time of seven years. Congratulations!" In this case, the professor won. But if he could not find a plausible explanation for the idiot's answer, the latter was declared the winner. I usually preferred the part of the idiot since it was easier. It was amazing, however, how much useful information I managed to accumulate, thanks to this curious little game.

In the evenings, I often wandered along the banks of the Moldau. The river was spanned by dozens of bridges which were embellished with statues of saints. In the distance, on top of a hill, loomed Hradčany castle, the ancient seat of Bohemian kings. The streets of the old city were gaslit and full of mystery. A boy of eleven could roam them at will and satiate his craving for adventure without fear of danger or bodily harm. Old Prague was full of ghosts, but theirs was a benign, almost protective, presence.

But all that was behind me now. Darkness had settled

over the chanting crowd below my window. The familiar melody of the anthem filled me with sadness. And then I heard a different sound: the unmistakable clatter of tanks. I recognized it from the year before on the Ringstrasse of Vienna. Suddenly, out of the gloom, the first German Panzer became visible. It rounded the corner and slowly, menacingly, rattled up St. Wenceslaus Square, toward the parliament building. It was followed by another and yet another, until the entire square was covered with gray-green Nazi tanks. The noise of their engines had almost drowned out the singing.

The tanks had pushed the crowd back toward the parliament building, the symbol of Czechoslovakia's sovereignty. The Czech policemen pleaded with their countrymen to give way, but to no avail. The crowd, thousands of chanting Czechs, stood fast, defiantly confronting their German conquerors. The noise of the idling Panzer engines mingled in macabre counterpoint with the final stanza of the Czech national anthem bursting forth from a thousand throats.

Suddenly, a lone woman with a kerchief around her head, clutching a little flag, stepped out of the crowd and slowly walked toward the lead tank. About halfway, she threw herself on the ground directly in the path of the giant Panzer. The crowd had stopped singing. And then silently, more women prostrated themselves, blocking the German advance. Within a few minutes, hundreds were lying facedown in the slush of St. Wenceslaus Square, literally covering the last bit of free Czech soil with their bodies. On a signal of the lead tank, the other Panzers rolled up until they confronted the desperate women in one massive row of power and steel. Then they lowered their guns. The women did not stir.

After a minute's hesitation, the lead tank aimed its gun at one of the Czech policemen standing by. A shot rang out. I saw the tall man in the blue uniform crumple to the ground. The tank fired two more volleys and two more policemen

fell over dead. A long and terrible silence descended over
the square. Suddenly, two small children approached one of
the prostrate women and tugged at her elbow. They seemed
to be pleading with her to rise. After a small struggle, the
woman obeyed and accompanied her children back into the
waiting crowd. The others quietly followed her example
and gave up the hopeless struggle. Slowly, heavily, hundreds
of women picked themselves up from the wet cobblestones
and shuffled back into the darkness. The showdown was
over. The Panzers raised their guns and resumed their advance toward the parliament. I was shaking. Between sobs,
I felt Mama's hand on my head. She had joined me at the
window.

"Do not forget this," she said. "Never forget." Then she
closed the window.

Mama had taken a lover. He was a tall man who looked
like a Prussian officer. And indeed, he had served as a
lieutenant in World War I and liked to tell a story about
how, on one occasion, he had seen the German kaiser.
Actually, he was a Jewish refugee from Germany and his
name was Oscar. He took an instant dislike to me which I
heartily reciprocated. Whenever he appeared at the apartment, he made me feel that I was in the way. He took almost all of Mama's time and I was left alone a great deal.

One day, Mama asked me with some embarrassment
whether I could bring myself to address her friend as Uncle
Oscar. I must have gone pale because she hugged me tightly.

But then she announced hesitantly: "I have decided to
marry him."

"Do you love him?" I asked, my heart pounding.

"He is in love with me," my mother answered.

"But do you love him?" I insisted. For a long time, Mama
did not reply.

Then she said, "These are bad times for us, terrible times. I am afraid to be alone. And you need a father."

"I am afraid of him," I said without thinking. The words had come out involuntarily. Cold with fear, I held on to my mother's hand.

"And I am afraid of Hitler," she said, reaching for my other hand. Thus we sat, huddled together, for a long time. Two weeks later, Oscar and Mama were married.

From that point on, my life went from bad to worse. Especially in school. Once more the classrooms were filled with uniformed Hitler Youth and again I was the outsider. Again, I suffered insults and beatings. Once, in the middle of a history class, there was a rough knock at the door. Six *Hitlerjugend* with swastika armbands and silver daggers stormed into the room, faced the class, saluted, and announced in unison: "All Jews must leave the school within the next five minutes." Our teacher, with rare presence of mind, pointed to a painting of Christ that was hanging on the wall and asked innocently, "Should he go, too?"

A blank stare was the answer.

I rose, got my belongings together, and walked to the door. The six Nazi boys, however, armed with rubber truncheons, were blocking the exit. Screaming with delight, they dragged me to the window and pushed me out. I landed in a pile of rubble a few feet below the window. Other Hitler Youths pulled me out and beat me till I was unconscious. Some hours later I awoke in the Jewish hospital covered with bruises. It seemed like Vienna all over again.

Life continued to get worse. When on the street, I was required to wear a yellow Star of David. I was not permitted to play in the park, to use a streetcar, ride in a cab, or to leave the house after six o'clock in the evening. At home, things weren't much better. Oscar had taken to beating me regularly for the slightest infraction of his Draconian house rules. Since our living quarters consisted of two small rooms, I was never more than a few feet from his glowering presence. I came to fear his brutality as much as that of the Nazis.

Mama, afraid to protect me against him, lapsed into a kind of passive melancholia and spent hours on end staring sightlessly at the walls. I spent as little time at home as possible. Whenever I could, I fled to my grandparents' home. There I felt loved and secure.

Sometimes, I would weep in my grandmother's arms. "Oscar is like Hitler," I blurted out once.

"Maybe that's why he understands him," my grandmother said cryptically, and then stared out the window in silence. I looked at her questioningly. Then she added mysteriously: "And perhaps that will save you."

On one occasion, I came home about fifteen minutes late. "Where have you been?" Oscar shouted.

"I tried to pick some wildflowers in the forest for Mama," I answered without thinking.

Oscar grumbled something but decided not to hit me. My mother smiled at me affectionately. The truth was that I hadn't looked for flowers; I had simply forgotten the time. But to admit that fact would have meant a vicious beating. It was easier to lie.

Gradually, lying to Oscar became second nature to me. On the other hand, I would do anything to please Mama so that she would protect me against Oscar. Between my lies to him and my efforts to manipulate my mother, the truth became a casualty. In my overriding search for safety, I gradually lost sight of everything else. Worse than that, I no longer knew quite who I was, save that I was a liar. And for that I was punished by a most effective weapon: a guilty conscience and a deepening conviction that Oscar was quite right when, in his rages, he would scream at me that I would come to a bad end.

Every Sunday, my grandparents would drive to a nursing

home in the outskirts of Prague to visit my ninety-year-old great-grandmother. Though quite frail, the old lady had retained a lucid mind and an extraordinary sense of humor. She prided herself on her agnosticism. Her closest companion in the home was an old Catholic woman of the Czech aristocracy who loved my great-grandmother but was eager to convert her.

"She told me yesterday that she will need a lady-in-waiting in heaven," great-grandmother said, wiping away tears of laughter, "and she has asked me to assist her in dressing for the resurrection."

One Sunday, however, I saw great-grandmother cry for the first time. She embraced my grandparents for a long time. The nursing home was to be closed and the inmates to be shipped to Theresienstadt.

"We will be with you soon," grandmother sobbed.

I tried my best to comfort her.

Mama looked more and more haggard, but I cherished the moments I spent alone with her. Whenever I heard Oscar's heavy footsteps on the stairs, my heart contracted with fear. Dinners usually took place in oppressive silence with only the most obligatory conversation.

Then one evening, Oscar looked at me across the table and announced coldly: "You had better pack your things. We are leaving Prague next week."

I looked at my mother, imploring her to explain.

"Uncle Oscar has been working very hard to get us a visa," Mama said uncertainly, reaching for my hand.

"Must we really go?" I choked out.

Oscar glared at me. He put both elbows on the table and said, "Yes, we must really go. Yes, there is no other choice. And no, your grandparents cannot come along. These three visas cost twenty thousand Reichsmark. All my money, all your mother's money." And then he added coldly, "And all your grandparents' money. So they *must* stay here. And they *will* stay here."

I stared at Oscar. For two years I had silently endured his beatings and his curses. But that was *me*. Now it was *them*, and it was too much. I loved my grandparents more than anything else in the world. Oscar had now committed the ultimate crime: He had bankrupted my grandparents and was separating Mama and me from them forever. He had plundered Omi's and Opi's savings, the fruit of forty years of labor. And our own.

All I could do was glare at him and shriek, "What? You can't. I—"

"Shut up, you little fool," he said angrily, cutting me off. "We have to get out. And there is very little time. The handwriting is on the wall. I know."

"It will pass," my mother suddenly cried out. "It will pass. You can't. We cannot—"

Oscar turned to her and froze her with a look of cold contempt. "Listen," he said, "these are illegal visas which are already paid for and which could cost us our lives. They have already cost us every cent we have. If one word of this leaks out from either of you, we will all die in a concentration camp. Do you understand?" he hissed at her.

"And you," he said, pointing his finger across the table at me, "you, I swear, if any word gets out, you I will kill personally. I swear I will do it myself."

His threat enraged my mother. "Oscar!" she shouted at him. "Stop!"

It was the first time I had ever heard Mama oppose Oscar. She was crying now, calling him "an adventurer" and shrieking that he had "bankrupted my family." At last, her hands pressed to her temples, she broke down into uncontrollable sobs and rushed out of the room.

Oscar and I sat there a long time, silent and alone. The only sounds were the ticking of the mantel clock and Oscar's labored breathing. He was working himself up into a terrible rage, and God only knew what would happen. The tiny room grew even smaller. Oscar's face was a mask of cold fury. But when he spoke to me, it was with an eerie softness. Between clenched teeth he said to me, "Someday you will thank me, you little bastard. Someday when the others are dead and you are alive, you will remember. You will remember that you owe me your life. God knows what you did to deserve it, but you will owe me that."

I stared at the table and said nothing.

Oscar continued, his voice still soft with menace, "The others are fools. They do not understand Hitler and his kind. But I do."

At that moment I feared Oscar as much as I feared Satan. Yet, I could not resist one more plea. I whispered, "Omi and Opi cannot go?"

The question fell into a void. In the other room Mama was wailing now. Oscar, his rage slowly subsiding, continued staring at me across the table, with haunted eyes.

"Then where are we going this time?" I asked, my voice starting to crack.

He was silent for a long moment and then said tonelessly, matter-of-factly, "To China."

I ran all the way to my grandparents' house. "I am not going, I am not going," I screamed, out of control. "Not without you." Grandfather took me by the hand and led me to the chessboard. It was no use. "I love you, I love you," I sobbed. "I can't leave without you."

"We love you too," said my grandfather, gently taking me in his arms, "and that's why you must go. We are old, Hitler can no longer harm us, but you must have a future."

"But why can't you go too?" I insisted.

"We couldn't get a visa. We are too old," grandfather replied tonelessly. His kind eyes glistened with tears behind the pince-nez. "You must be strong and brave now," he said. "You are thirteen, almost a man."

Gratefully, I looked at him. "And where is China?" I asked.

The old man put his arm around my shoulder and led me to a map that was hanging on the wall in his study. Slowly, he traced the route to China with his finger. "It is on the other side of the world," he said calmly.

The day of our departure drew nearer. The journey to China was to take us across Siberia and Japan. Our final destination was to be Shanghai, China's largest city. Mama had told me that it was the only place in the entire world to which Oscar had been able to get us an entrance visa. Oscar and Mama were busy packing. I was told to pack a small suitcase. Only essentials could go, Oscar explained, and nothing of value could be taken across the German border. I prayed that something would happen to wake me from what I believed to be a nightmare. But the nightmare was reality.

Finally, the day had arrived. It fell on Mama's birthday, in March 1941. We were to board a train for Moscow that night. Grandmother prepared dinner but only Oscar ate. During the meal, when Oscar wasn't looking, grandmother handed Mama her prize possession: a large diamond brooch framed in an antique platinum setting. My mother quickly slipped the heirloom in her purse.

At dusk, Oscar hailed a taxi and asked the driver to take us to the station. Since Mama and Oscar looked German, no questions were asked. My grandparents were to follow in another taxi, to bid us farewell.

As we drove through Prague for that last time, it occurred to me that we were violating at least three anti-Jewish laws: We were out after six, weren't wearing our yellow stars, and were traveling by taxi. Desperately, I hoped that we would be stopped.

But we reached the station without incident. Passengers

were already boarding the Moscow train, and a conductor took us to our assigned compartment. We quickly climbed aboard with our bags. Immediately, I lowered the window and looked up and down the platform, hoping to find my grandparents. They were nowhere to be seen.

The train was scheduled to leave at eight o'clock. The large station clock showed seven forty-five. My mother was desperate with anguish. I, too, was frantic. Neither one of us had said goodbye. Oscar sat impassively. My eyes darted from the platform to the minute hand on the station clock. At five minutes to eight I finally saw my grandparents.

"Here we are," I shouted. They heard me and came running to the train window. I knew it was against the rules, but I no longer cared. I turned around, dashed to the exit, and jumped off the train, into my grandmother's arms. Oscar's face appeared at the open window, contorted with rage.

"I am not going with you," I screamed at the top of my lungs. "You are not my father. I am staying here."

Two SS officers, startled by the commotion, looked at me with idle curiosity.

"Then go and kill yourself, you bastard, like your father did," Oscar hissed under his breath.

It was two minutes past eight. The train began to move. With all his strength, my grandfather picked me up and put me on the moving train. Mama pulled me in. I looked back into the night. A flashlight was moving in the distance, up and down, up and down. Then it was gone.

The train chugged through the night. I peered out the window. The snowy landscape rushed by, serene and tranquil in the moonlight. Oscar was snoring. Mama, after taking a sedative, had fallen into a fitful slumber. I wanted to ask her whether what Oscar had said about Papa was true, but I was afraid to wake her. The grief of leaving my grandparents kept me from sleeping, so I counted the little Czech villages as the train steamed toward Poland. Then I remembered what the geography teacher had told us: There was no more Poland and the German Reich now shared a common border with the Soviet Union.

Toward morning the door of our compartment opened. I was almost dozing and did not see the man who entered. My first view of him was at floor level and that was enough to make me choke. For what I saw was a pair of black military boots. Then I heard two words that made my heart race with terror: "Heil Hitler!"—followed without a second's hesitation by an equally emphatic "Heil Hitler!"

When I looked up, I saw Oscar. Incredibly, he had jumped up and was saluting. He had returned the man's "Heil Hitler" with the precision and authority of a well-trained German officer.

Then I looked at the man whom Oscar had saluted.

Standing in the compartment door was a man in Wehrmacht uniform. It was not just any uniform, but the awesome, beribboned dress tunic of a high-ranking Nazi officer. A Wehrmacht colonel was about to join us in our journey to the Soviet Union.

Shaken by fear and nausea, I wondered whether Oscar's reaction was a reflex from his war years or whether it was an act, an example of his instinct for survival. Either way, the scene was ghastly: Oscar frozen in a stiff salute, Hitler's name, spoken proudly, on his lips. It seemed that alongside the Wehrmacht colonel, Oscar was now in his true element.

Almost immediately Oscar produced a bottle of rare cognac that Omi and Opi had given us and offered a toast to the Führer. And then another toast, and yet another. It all seemed like a hideous joke. Three homeless Jews were fleeing from the Holocaust and my stepfather was toasting the Third Reich with a Wehrmacht officer. I sat there paralyzed and listened to their war stories, and watched them drink and toast and even sing. I thought of Omi and Opi abandoned to the Nazis. Oscar might as well have toasted Satan.

And yet, this man I hated with a black bottomless hate was saving my life and the life of my helpless mother. So visible was our grief that the colonel's suspicions would almost certainly have been aroused. But Oscar's *Sieg Heils* were so utterly convincing that the colonel soon regarded us as friends and allies. He leaned toward Oscar and whispered with a conspiratorial smile, "When the time comes, we shall squeeze the life out of those Bolshevik dogs. Our Führer knows exactly what to do." His large hands were choking an imaginary Bolshevik. Exhausted, he leaned back in his corner. "I wonder when they will serve us breakfast on this train," he then muttered, to no one in particular.

Oscar opened a paper bag and offered it to the colonel. I noticed that it contained the last Prague supper, carefully wrapped in wax paper—several pieces of fried chicken and some potato salad. Oscar and his Nazi friend hungrily consumed every last morsel.

As I watched the two men eat, I fell into a terrible despair. I began to cry quietly, and when the colonel asked me what was wrong, I could only sob, "Omi and Opi," and then, "Papa, Papa."

I knew immediately that I had made a terrible mistake by losing control over my feelings and that Oscar was now livid with rage. So I suppressed my tears and kept quiet, as Oscar glared at me.

Eventually the colonel fell asleep and began to snore. Oscar got up from his seat and walked over to my corner.

"Come with me," he commanded in a voice that brooked no opposition. Numb with fear, I obeyed. Oscar's drinking with the Wehrmacht colonel had terrified me.

Silently, I followed him out of the compartment, down the corridor. He opened the door of the men's toilet and ordered me to enter. After looking over his shoulder, he followed me in, quickly pulling the door shut behind him.

Then he turned toward me, eyes blazing with a murderous fury. The blows came quickly and hard. Soon my nose was bleeding and I was sobbing with terror. But my screams were drowned out by the noise of the train.

"Listen, you bastard, and listen well," Oscar hissed between clenched teeth. "I have told them you are my son, because your mother didn't want to leave you behind. Your father is dead. If you mention his name, I will kill you with my bare hands." Oscar's large hands made a choking motion. More quietly he added, "Don't you understand that if you travel under a different name, the Germans will ask questions and we will all be killed?" His voice rising again, he asked, "Do you have anything on you that bears your father's name?"

Trembling, I pulled out a faded photograph of Papa that I had carried around in my pocket for years.

"Hand it over," Oscar commanded. He tore the little memento out of my hand, and flushed it down the toilet.

"Anything else?" he barked.

I was silent.

He hit me again.

"Anything else?" he repeated.

I shook my head. All I had left of Papa had been flushed down a train toilet somewhere in Poland. Then I looked at Oscar. I hated him, but I realized that I owed him my life. Perhaps he was right. I would have to give up Papa. Now it was Oscar or Hitler. Something in me contracted icily. I was on my own.

We returned to the compartment. The colonel had awakened and greeted Oscar like a long lost friend. The train was beginning to slow down. Mama seemed nervous and kept fidgeting with her purse. Suddenly, she opened it and took out grandmother's diamond brooch. After a moment's hesitation, she lowered the compartment window and threw the shiny object out into the dawn. No one had noticed anything. My mother sat down heavily, her face buried in her hands.

Shortly afterward, a Nazi border official entered. "Passports, please!" he announced. The colonel grunted something and handed the man a piece of paper with a large swastika embossed on it in gold. The official sprang to attention and saluted stiffly. Then Oscar handed him a document.

"Your son?" The official waved in my direction.

Oscar nodded.

"Open the luggage," the Nazi commanded, raking Oscar with a hard suspicious stare. Oscar nervously reached for the nearest suitcase. He was aware that all families leaving Germany were viewed with suspicion.

"*Heraus!*" the Wehrmacht colonel screamed suddenly in a military tone. "They are my friends."

"*Jawohl*, Herr Obersturmbannführer!" The border guard clicked his heels and fled from the compartment with an obsequious bow. Soon afterward, the train rolled into the border station. The colonel whom Oscar had courted so successfully got off after kissing Mama's hand.

I looked out the window. The small station seemed to be divided into two separate parts. On the left, there was a picture of Hitler, draped with a swastika. On the right fluttered a crimson banner which adorned the portrait of a kindly looking elderly man with a mustache.

"Who is that?" I wanted to know.

"Stalin," replied Oscar. "And don't ask any more questions."

A Soviet customs official came in and glanced at our bags. "Is that all?" he asked.

Oscar nodded again. The man stamped the suitcases and left.

Suddenly, Mama began to cry hysterically. She was still sobbing when the train began to move. Stalin's picture floated by, smiling benignly.

"At last a free country," Oscar said.

Chapter Three

The Trans-Siberian express was a comfortable train. We had boarded it in Moscow and now, after ten days of travel punctuated by occasional brief stops, we had crossed the Urals and were traversing Siberia. I sat near the window and gazed at the landscape. Gradually, forests gave way to snow-covered tundra. The high northern latitude, the extreme slant of the rays of the wintry sun, the flatness of the terrain—all these combined to accent the horizontal at the expense of the vertical and to create everywhere a sense of immense space, distance, and power. The heaven was vast, the skyline remote and extended. I felt the proximity of the great wilderness of the Russian North—silent, somber, infinitely patient. The white moonlit nights had an unbelievable eerie poetry. Their loneliness resonated with mine.

Once a day, while the train was taking on coal, we were allowed to get off and exercise by walking briskly up and down the station platform of some remote Siberian town. The temperature was arctic.

"Don't pee in the snow!" warned the friendly old conductor who seemed to be a relic from the days of the czar, "or your little thing will turn into an icicle."

Old grandmothers with weather-beaten faces tried to sell

us goats' milk and hard-boiled eggs. In Irkutsk, a whole detachment of soldiers got on the train. They were good-natured and one of them played the harmonica for me. To the intense displeasure of the meticulous Oscar, a Red Army officer kept urinating into the washbasin. He did so from a measured distance, with amazing precision, and with consummate artistry. Oscar glared at him, but said nothing. The officer grinned back broadly.

Four weeks after we had left Moscow, the train pulled into Vladivostok, on the Soviet Pacific coast. There we waited for three more weeks for a fishing vessel to carry us to Japan. I met a young Russian Orthodox priest. He took a liking to me and we took long walks together on the docks of Vladivostok harbor.

"Over there is Alaska and America," he said, pointing across the Bering Sea. "Is that where you will be going?"

"No," I replied, wishing I could answer yes, "we are heading for China."

A small boat dropped us at the Japanese port of Kobe and it took another month for a Chinese cargo ship to carry us to Shanghai. When we finally disembarked among a horde of coolies, rickshaws, and dock workers, it was late June 1941. The heat was stifling. I looked around in bewilderment. A newspaper headline at a nearby stand caught my eye: "Germany Invades Russia," it said. I was frightened. Hitler seemed to be following us halfway around the world.

One hundred years before we had landed in Shanghai, the colorful Chinese port had been divided up among several Western nations. Each of these foreign countries had carved out a part of the city for itself which it regarded virtually as its property. Thus, one section resembled an English provincial town, and prided itself on a main street named after Queen Victoria and a British public school for boys in which I was enrolled. Adjacent to it, there was a French "concession" in which Oscar and Mama rented a modest apartment and where Oscar found a job as teller in an import-export bank. On the other side there was the German settlement with a high school named after Kaiser Wilhelm. The Chinese were generally reduced to second-class status in these foreign sections and forced to live in the slums. Chinese law did not apply in any of the "extraterritorial settlements." Instead, the English teachers at the public school taught us Rudyard Kipling's "White Man's Burden." I was told that I would have to study English, French, and Chinese. Fortunately, I had a musical ear and languages came easily to me. Life was bearable again. Oscar had even stopped beating me.

But one day in December this colonial splendor came to a sudden end. The Japanese had attacked the United States at Pearl Harbor and Shanghai came under Japanese martial law. The German community prevailed on its Japanese allies to round up all Jews and force them to move into a ghetto. Oscar lost his job, the little apartment had to be given up, and we moved into a one-room flat. The ghetto was surrounded by barbed wire and guarded by Japanese sentries with fierce police dogs. Swastikas became visible all over the German settlement and the Kaiser Wilhelm School was renamed after Adolf Hitler.

Mama began to cry again. One day she became hysterical. A letter had arrived from my grandparents. It had been mailed from Theresienstadt and had taken six months to reach China. They wrote that they had been deported from Prague four weeks after our departure. Mama feared for their lives.

Oscar had nothing to do and had taken to beating me again. I almost felt sorry for him. He had saved us from Hitler and had brought us halfway across the world. And here we were, still in Hitler's power, in a Jewish ghetto in China.

The ghetto school which I attended offered a strange

mixture of excellence and brutality. Many of the British and French teachers, stranded in Shanghai and unable to go home, decided to wait out the war by teaching us Shakespeare and Voltaire. I immersed myself in *Hamlet* and acted the part of the Danish prince in a school play, imagining that King Claudius was Oscar. I gave a creditable performance. The hatreds of the war were reflected among the pupils. Racial tensions were rampant and beatings were common. On one occasion, a number of boys had torn off my shirt and were taking turns at hitting me with a bamboo cane. The biggest of the bullies offered the cane to a Russian boy standing nearby and ordered him to join in the beating.

"Hit him, or you will get the same medicine," he was told.

The frail Russian took the piece of bamboo, broke it in half, and crossed his arms. From that moment on, Rusty and I became inseparable.

Rusty was a quiet, fair-haired boy with a gift for drawing and painting. Like myself, he was somewhat of a loner. But unlike myself, he was deeply religious. Rusty could talk for hours about the nature of God.

"Before you are born," he said one night, "God sorts out your soul. If you've got a round soul, he puts you on a round planet; if you've got an oval soul, he puts you on an oval planet."

"So what's your soul like?" I wanted to know.

"In my case, God made a mistake," Rusty said sadly. "I've got an oval soul, and he put me on a round planet. And the school keeps trying to file my soul round like everyone else's."

Rusty's favorite writer was the French aviator Antoine de Saint-Exupéry, whose *Little Prince* was published in the middle of the war. Rusty was fascinated by the sad little boy who was the ruler and sole inhabitant of asteroid B-612. When we learned in 1944 that the flier had not returned from a mission over his Nazi-occupied homeland, Rusty was inconsolable. "He's gone to look for the little prince," he said.

Rusty's mother was a prostitute who lived in a two-room flat near the ghetto. She said that she had been married to a Russian count who had been killed during the Bolshevik revolution. Rusty's own origins were a mystery. We would sit with her in the afternoons before she went to work, and she would pour us endless cups of tea from a large pot-bellied samovar. Then she would examine my palms and tell my future. It was always the same: I would go to America after the war and make my fortune.

Rusty assured me that his mother was a palmist of excellent reputation. She had predicted a fine future for him in Australia. We trusted her implicitly but begged her to tell us if there was a way for us to stay together.

"No," she said mockingly, "and you should be grateful that I don't predict your death by an American bomb."

At least once a week, Shanghai was subjected to aerial bombardment. The American B-29s aimed at the Japanese military installations on the outskirts of the city, but not infrequently they missed and hit the ghetto instead. There were few air raid shelters since the city was built on swampland. There was no place to hide and often Rusty and I would look up at the attacking planes and wish that we could fly back with them to America.

As the raids increased in ferocity, I spent less and less time at home since Oscar and my mother were more miserable now than ever. Sometimes, Rusty and I would sit in his little room and talk about God. I had become confused by the fact that each army in the war appealed for victory to the same God. Perhaps God was an old general with a vast closet full of different uniforms, spending all his time changing from one into another and then rushing off to lead an army. I felt sorry for him. It seemed to be a thankless job.

Rusty was attracted to spiritualism and one night, during a particularly violent raid, we tried to conjure up the spirits of our dead fathers. Nothing happened. Rusty explained this by saying that he had no likeness of his father and therefore was unable to conjure up his image. I tried to conjure up Papa's face from the memory of the faded photograph that Oscar had flushed down the train toilet, but to no avail. Papa did not appear. Instead, the all-clear sounded and we crept up on the roof of the whorehouse, to shoot down Japanese planes. The objective was to get an erection as quickly as possible while lying on our backs. We aimed our weapons at the gray dawn above the city and dozens of planes fell out of the sky. By morning, our depression had vanished.

Rusty and I were the only virgins left in our class. We were sixteen by now and consumed by sexual urgency. I wrote poetry and was told by the teacher that I had considerable talent. Some of my classmates felt that my poetry would improve even further if I could draw on some real experience for my love poems. An Indian student who prided himself on his sexual exploits took up a collection for me among my classmates for a visit to the neighborhood brothel. After consulting with Rusty, I acquiesced reluctantly. Rusty advised that an hour of conversation should be included in the price so that I could benefit from the experience as a poet.

The bordellos of Shanghai, like the schools, mirrored the racial divisions of the war. Chinese girls were readily available and fetched the lowest fees. They catered largely to the enlisted men of the Japanese occupation army. Some of the more exclusive downtown brothels which serviced German businessmen and high Japanese army officers supplied white women of uncertain age and ancestry. These ladies prided themselves on their French or Russian accents and alleged links to the European nobility. Chinese money had become almost worthless. Rates changed daily, often hourly, and always up. It was not unusual to carry around a suitcase full of paper currency. Sometimes the prices changed while one waited in line to pay. Barter was also common. Negotiations for bordello services were no exception.

On the appointed day, I marched down to the bordello, accompanied by ten financial contributors, all of whom were eager to witness the results of my practical education. Sarkari, the Indian entrepreneur, had chosen the Golden Dragon for me. The Golden Dragon was a good-natured Chinese whore who weighed more than two hundred pounds and prided herself on a row of golden teeth and an enormous posterior. On slow evenings, the Golden Dragon would bet a client on whether she could pull a nail out of the wall with her buttocks. It was said that considerable sums had changed hands on such nights and that it was prudent to wager on the side of the Dragon. Sarkari assured me that an hour's conversation had been negotiated: half an hour before and half an hour after. Rusty slipped me a nail file. "In case she becomes dangerous," he said affectionately.

We arrived at the house. Business seemed brisk and none of the whores were visible on the veranda. Sarkari rang the bell and Ma, the corpulent madam, appeared at the door. Sarkari flashed his most seductive smile but Ma waved him away with a peremptory gesture. It seemed that something had gone wrong. After another appeal, Sarkari walked over to me and announced glumly, "Prices have gone up again because of inflation. You can fuck her, but you can't talk to her. There is no time for the scheduled conversation." After a hurried consultation, we gave in. Things had gone too far, and there was no turning back.

Trying to hide my nervousness, I followed the Golden Dragon up the stairs while the contributors waited below. I had dressed for the occasion in my only good suit and was perspiring profusely. The Dragon smiled her golden smile, walked over to me and loosened my tie. She slipped out of her dress and enormous rolls of fat cascaded down over her hips. Stark naked, she began to take off my shirt. Frantic with fear, I pointed toward three whips which were hang-

ing on the wall. They reminded me of those in the headmaster's office at school and seemed to be the only possible
topic of conversation. I was desperate to avert a complete
fiasco although I knew that my initiation, with or without
conversation, was in serious jeopardy. The Dragon, noticing
my diversionary maneuver, took one of the whips off the
wall and lashed me gently across the flanks. She is becoming
dangerous, I thought, remembering Rusty's nail file. I pulled
out the little weapon and pointed it at the Dragon. The
woman looked at my hand and stopped smiling. Instead,
she hit me hard with the whip and pushed me toward the
door with a violent curse.

"Out," she screamed at the top of her lungs. "Out, you
crazy little bastard!"

I stumbled down the stairs. The Dragon, still cursing,
threw my shirt and tie down after me. Then she slammed
the door.

"What the hell happened?" asked Sarkari. I must have
looked like death. His voice betrayed genuine concern.

"She lashed me with a whip," I managed to stammer.

"You idiot," Sarkari laughed, "she probably thought you
were a masochist and wanted to do you a favor." I didn't
know what he was talking about.

"Don't tell the others," I begged.

The shame almost choked me. Rusty came up and put his
arm around me. I gave him back his nail file and told him
everything. When I had finished, Rusty looked thoughtful.

"The same thing would have happened to me," he said.
"I think you and I must be in love before we can do it. And
it's not going to happen to us here."

I looked at him gratefully. We walked away together,
and began to talk about America.

In the spring of 1945, my mother suffered a nervous
breakdown and had to enter a hospital. She had learned that

sometime during 1944 my grandparents had been transported to Auschwitz and that they had perished there. I tried to comfort her but she was inconsolable. The guilt for leaving her parents behind consumed her. Oscar was now alone in the little one-room flat. I had moved in with Rusty. On occasion, his mother needed our room for a special customer. At such times we roamed the outskirts of the city, hunting for mulberry leaves.

Rusty and I had a few silkworms on the windowsill and the only food they ate was the leaf of the mulberry tree. The worms crawled around our wooden box, eating ravenously. After a few weeks they would shed their iridescent skins so that they could continue to grow. Then, one day, they would spin a white or pink cocoon of pure silk. Within a month, a moth would emerge. The moths would live only for a week. Eating nothing, all they did was copulate.

Fascinated, we paired them off and watched them glued together in the act of reproduction. Shortly afterward, the female moths would swell up and lay hundreds of little yellow eggs the size of pinheads. Then the moths died, but as soon as the weather became warm again, the eggs would pop and tiny worms would wriggle out.

Now it was May and a few of the worms had just begun to work on their cocoons. One day, Rusty rushed in, breathlessly waving a newspaper.

"Hitler is dead!" he shouted.

We did not sleep that night. We knew now that the war could not last too much longer.

The summer of 1945 was terrible. Order was breaking down. Shanghai was the last remaining major city under Japanese military occupation. Food was scarce and many people were starving. The American bombers paid us nightly visits and made sleep impossible. School was suspended and Rusty and I roamed the streets, looking for food.

In August, a rumor swept through the city that the Americans had dropped a horrible new bomb on Japan. Mass hysteria broke out. Rape, pillage, and murder became commonplace. A typhus epidemic erupted. One day, I developed a raging fever and Rusty brought me to the local hospital. The doctor diagnosed typhus.

For several days, I hovered between life and death. The hospital was under quarantine and packed with typhus patients. The beds were so close together that there was hardly any room to walk between them. On the bed to my right lay an elderly man, his cheeks hollowed out by fever and starvation. He was so weak that he was unable to move.

"Play with yourself," he whispered to me. "So long as you can get it up, you won't die."

The next day he was dead and an orderly carried off his body. I concentrated on the girl's face that I would love but that I had never seen and followed the dead man's instructions. Two weeks later the fever had subsided and I was released from the hospital.

The war was finally over. Rusty and I went to the highway and watched the Japanese occupation force pull out. Two weeks later, Chinese soldiers of Chiang Kai-shek's army marched into the city. They were not impressive victors. They looked starved and exhausted and wore torn boots caked with mud. The soldiers descended on the city like locusts, foraging for food. It was rumored that a few hundred miles away, a Chinese Communist army was getting ready to advance. Its leader was a man named Mao Tse-tung.

American uniforms began to appear in town. I attached myself to an American lieutenant who regarded me as a kind of mascot. Then I landed a job as a dock worker unloading relief supplies. Finally, I managed to get a job as interpreter in the Shanghai office of the newly established United Nations Relief and Rehabilitation Administration. My heart swelled with pride. I had heard of the creation of the United Nations at San Francisco.

I asked my boss whether he could use another boy. He

nodded and I ran to Rusty's house. Now we were able to work side by side. We earned weekly wages, ate well, and were determined to make Rusty's prophecy come true.

I tried my best, through UNRRA, to trace the fate of my grandparents. I clung to the hope that perhaps, by some miracle, they might have escaped the gas ovens of Auschwitz after all. I found out that they had been shot—together with several thousand other elderly Jews—standing at the edge of a pit that was to become their grave. In horror, I wondered what their last moment might have been. Did they speak? Did they pray? Did they cling to one another? Did they take one last look at the sky? Two good people who had loved me and who had never harmed anyone; dying, they fell on top of corpses and other corpses fell on top of them. They are still falling.

My mother and Oscar continued to live in the ghetto, but I visited them only rarely. Oscar had no job and I gave them a part of my wages every week. My mother and I had become estranged. I could not forgive her for having married Oscar, and Oscar could not forgive me for existing. Several times I asked my mother whether it was true that Papa had killed himself. Once, she nodded, but when I pressed her for details, she looked away and refused to answer. Oscar stared at me with undisguised hatred. But despite his jealousy, he no longer beat me. He had become afraid.

One day, a jovial American dropped into our UNRRA office. He was introduced to me as Charles Jordan of the Jewish Joint Distribution Committee. Mr. Jordan found it amusing that I was able to recite the part of Hamlet by heart. Would you be interested in a scholarship to an American college? he asked. Would I be interested? I would have signed a pact with the devil. Mr. Jordan looked at me kindly and asked me to show him my school reports. They were excellent. The headmaster had certified that I had received only two canings for misconduct, and that I excelled in the English language and showed promise in French and

Chinese. Mr. Jordan was impressed and promised that he would try his best for me.

For three months I waited in a fever of anticipation. And then, in late 1946, Mr. Jordan walked in and announced that I had been admitted to a small college in the American Middle West with a full scholarship.

"It's called Grinnell," he said, "and it's in a state called Iowa. A very famous American actor named Gary Cooper went there."

Unable to speak, I reached for Mr. Jordan's hand.

"All you need now is a visa and passage on a boat," he added with a smile.

Getting the documents together was no easy task. Countless papers were required. The fact that I was stateless and had no passport made everything more difficult. The International Refugee Organization gave me a piece of paper which certified that I in fact existed. Then I laid siege to the American consulate where I was informed that if I wished to go to the United States as a regular immigrant I would have to wait until the year 2050. The Austrian quota was heavily oversubscribed. But, the consul added, it was possible to go to America as a student. He would agree to give me a student visa, but I would have to sign that I would return to my place of birth or most recent residence after the expiration of my studies. I signed the document without hesitation. I would have signed anything. Then I got myself a passage as a deckhand on a converted troop transporter, the *General Gordon*, which was to set sail for San Francisco in August 1947.

I had decided not to tell my mother about my good fortune. I was afraid that she would tell Oscar and that he would sabotage my plans.

Rusty, of course, knew everything. He had secured passage to Australia in exchange for pledging to work there as a laborer for two years. We reported our respective progress to Rusty's mother. Our admiration for her clairvoyant gifts had become unbounded. She, however, told us to keep working. "Lady Fortune is kind to those," she liked to say, "who do not rely on her too much." Rusty's mother had aged during the war and had lost most of her clients. Rusty shared his income with her.

I did not quite know how to break the news of my imminent departure to Mama and Oscar. The *General Gordon* was scheduled to leave in forty-eight hours. All my travel documents were in order and I had already quit my job. I had to pack my few belongings and could no longer hide my plans.

I climbed up the stairs of the ghetto flat for the last time and announced calmly, "I am going to America tomorrow."

Mama seemed stunned. "But what about me?" she asked fearfully.

"Mama," I said, "I have the chance to get an education at an American college."

My mother smiled and her eyes lit up with joy. I had not seen her smile like that for years.

"God bless you, my prince," she said softly. "You will find your happiness and fortune in America."

"Why didn't you tell us earlier?" Oscar asked. His voice trembled with a hidden fury. I did not answer. Oscar jumped to his feet. "You are a liar and a criminal," he shrieked, lunging at me. I stepped aside. "You will end in the gutter, like your father. The curse is in your blood and even America cannot wash it clean. Go to hell."

With all my heart I hoped that Mama would say something to defend me. But she kept silent. I left the house with a heavy heart.

Rusty had come to the dock to bid me farewell. He was to embark for Australia within a month. We had sustained each other through the war years and given each other the love we needed to stay alive. Now, we were unable to speak. It was six o'clock in the morning and the ship was scheduled to depart at seven. American soldiers were kissing their girls before boarding.

"Your mother was right," I managed to say through my tears. Then Rusty handed me a parting gift: a wooden sign with my name on it, neatly emblazoned in his artistic hand.

"My mother predicts that you will be working for the United Nations someday," Rusty said. "I made you a desk sign so that you will remember me." We embraced a long time. I gave Rusty my stamp collection, the only thing of value that I owned. We promised to write; then I went on board. Soon afterward, a siren sounded and the ship began to move downriver. Standing on the dock, Rusty looked alone and forlorn. I felt guilty that I couldn't take him with me. I waved to him, and he waved back with a blue handkerchief. Then I could no longer see him. The tall buildings of the Shanghai waterfront appeared in stark silhouette against the light of early morning. I cried with happiness and pain. The sun broke through the clouds as the ship moved out into the open sea.

Chapter Four

I enjoyed my duties as an auxiliary seaman on the *General Gordon*. In the mornings I scrubbed down the promenade deck, put up chairs for the first-class passengers, and served refreshments from the ship's bar. In the afternoons, I helped to peel potatoes in the kitchen and set the tables in the dining room. During the second half of the two-week voyage, I was promoted to waiter and earned tips from the dinner guests. In the evenings, I mingled with the American soldiers who were returning home from the war. I listened to their stories but was reluctant to ask questions. I was ashamed of betraying my ignorance about their homeland. The America I knew was a land of fantasy and dreams where I had sought refuge from a horrible reality. Slowly, I began to understand that this wonderland, too, had a geography with teeming cities called New York, San Francisco, and Chicago, and that Americans were not Olympian gods but mortal men and women with a normal range of human emotions. I was astounded at their capacity for drinking liquor and the size of the tips I pocketed. But some of the curses I heard during a midnight barroom brawl added a new dimension to my already quite extensive storehouse of profanity.

At night, when I was unable to sleep in the crowded steerage quarters, I would climb up on the lower deck and gaze out at the gently rolling sea. During the last days of the voyage, some of the soldiers taught me craps and poker. On the night before our arrival in San Francisco, several poker games were in progress. Unable to sleep, I wandered from one makeshift table to another, watching intently.

"Want me to deal you in, kid?" one of the soldiers asked. He was flipping cards around a wooden box to six or seven other players.

"Sure," I said without hesitation. Suddenly, my entire body began to vibrate with a powerful thrill that I had never felt before. It was as if someone had turned on an electric switch inside me. Seeing that each player had a stack of chips in front of him, I pulled out a hundred dollars and handed it to the soldier with the biggest pile. It was all the money I had made in tips during the last two weeks.

The soldier looked up briefly and flicked twenty chips in my direction. I was in the game.

During the next two hours the cards I was dealt were miserable. Too afraid to bluff, I folded one hand after another. My pile of chips was dwindling. Finally, at about four o'clock in the morning, an older soldier with a huge black beard dealt me an ace. I pushed two chips toward the center of the table and received a second ace. Two more chips went into the pot. The third card was a ten, and the fourth another ten. Only three of us were left in the game: the cook, the soldier with the beard, and I. I glanced at the pot; it contained well over three hundred dollars. The beard dealt the last card facedown. A third ten! I had a full house. The cook folded his hand with a curse.

"Your bet," said the beard, looking at me. I hesitated. Beads of sweat had formed on my forehead and the palms of my hands felt clammy as I pushed two more chips away from me.

The beard had watched me carefully. Suddenly, he said

calmly, "Raise you a hundred," and threw ten large chips into the pot. I looked at him in consternation, but his face behind the beard betrayed no emotion. He had raised me the limit. It would cost me a hundred dollars to stay in the game. My entire fortune consisted of one hundred and twenty dollars. I trembled. If I called the hand and lost, I would arrive in San Francisco virtually penniless. If I folded, all I would lose were my earnings. I could not take the chance.

"You win," I said. The beard raked in the pot.

"What did you have?" he asked.

"A full house."

He looked at me with disbelief. "In this game, you need balls, kid," he said, turning over his five cards. All I saw was a pair of queens. He had bluffed me out.

Stomach churning, I went to the latrine. I had suddenly developed a violent diarrhea. As I sat there, lost in thought, the door opened. It was the beard, still chewing on the same cigar as when he was playing cards.

"Listen, son," he said, sitting down with a groan, "I will tell you a story. The shithouse here reminds me of it." I looked up expectantly, my pain subsiding a little.

"I knew a guy who had lost his last dime in a casino in Nevada," the beard began, "he felt so bad he thought he was going to shit right in his pants. He just made it to the men's room, but then couldn't get his ass on the can because he needed a nickel. It was one of those goddamn pay toilets. Then he saw a guy washing his hands at the sink. 'Brother, can you lend me a nickel?' my friend asked in desperation. The man at the sink fished out a nickel, handed it over without a word, and left. My friend was about to put the nickel into the slot that would open the door, but then he noticed that it was open. He went in, did his business, and went back into the casino, looking for the man who had given him the nickel. He was nowhere to be seen. So my friend put the nickel into a slot machine. He hit the jackpot. With the winnings, he went back to the craps table and made another killing. But this time, he was smart. He quit, took his money, bought himself a partnership in a corporation, and became a business tycoon. But every afternoon at five o'clock my friend would say to his partner, 'I have to leave now, I have to find that man!'" The beard interrupted his story and looked at me. "Which man do you think my friend was looking for?" he asked.

"The man who gave him the nickel," I answered, without thinking.

"Wrong," said the beard, roaring with laughter. "The man who left the shithouse door open!"

Despite my pain, I had to laugh. I didn't get the point of the story, but I laughed so hard that the tears came. Then I went up on deck, feeling better. Daylight was breaking.

"There she is," said the beard, who had followed me up. He pointed into the distance. Against the dawn, barely visible, was the outline of a graceful arc. "There she is, the Golden Gate," the beard repeated. "We are home."

Two hours later, we steamed into San Francisco Bay. As we passed the Golden Gate Bridge, the beard put his arm on my shoulder and said: "Throw a penny into the sea; it will bring you luck." I threw a penny over the ship's railing. Suddenly, I had to think of Rusty who would soon be embarking for Australia.

"Jesus," said the beard suddenly. I looked up. A huge "Welcome Home" sign had become visible in the harbor. The soldiers were cheering. A large crowd had gathered on the dock and women were waving handkerchiefs. I thought of Rusty's lonesome figure receding into the distance on the docks of Shanghai. It seemed like years ago. The *General Gordon* docked, and we disembarked. When I stepped off the ship, I fell to the ground.

"Are you okay?" a voice behind me asked. It was the beard. He was smoking the longest cigar I had ever seen.

"I am fine," I answered, rising quickly. I did not want him to know that I had fallen to the ground on purpose to kiss the American soil.

Grinnell College was a small school in the heartland of the United States. I arrived there on a beautiful autumn evening in late September and was welcomed by a kind elderly lady who introduced herself as the housemother of the dormitory which was to be my home. She was just comforting a boy from a neighboring town, who had an attack of homesickness.

"Where are you from?" she asked, turning to me.

"Shanghai," I said.

"Shanghai, what?" Mrs. Hall wanted to know.

"China," I blurted out.

Mrs. Hall looked at me for a moment in disbelief, but said nothing. Then she opened the door to a small room with a window that overlooked a row of elm trees.

"We are a small college," she said, "but we pride ourselves on our high standards." I listened respectfully as Mrs. Hall opened the window of my room to let in the evening breeze. "We do not allow any drinking, there must be absolute quiet in the house after ten o'clock, and girls must be in their dormitories by eleven."

"What girls?" I asked. Ma's bordello in Shanghai had flashed through my mind.

"We have about five hundred girls on campus," Mrs. Hall explained. "Once a month there are chaperoned dances. On those occasions, you may keep your date out until midnight; after that, she is punished and turns into a pumpkin." Mrs. Hall laughed innocently. I stared at her uncomprehendingly.

"If you are homesick, please feel free to talk to me," she said gently, "and be sure to attend chapel on Sundays. And now you had better go to dinner," she added with a smile. "You look as if you could stand a decent meal."

Dinner was served in a large communal hall where I had the opportunity to meet my fellow students. Most of them were clean-cut young boys from midwestern towns who were away from home for the first time. The food was good. There was fried chicken, mountains of mashed potatoes, and cornbread, all of which was washed down with large pitchers of ice-cold milk. Dessert consisted of apple pie with vanilla ice cream. I ate everything and decided to take two containers of milk to my room for the night. One could not be sure, after all, if all that milk might not run out.

My academic adviser, to whom I was introduced the following morning, was the only Jewish faculty member on campus. Professor Joseph Dunner had come to the United States from Germany in 1938, as a refugee from Hitler. He was a thoughtful man with a leonine mane who enjoyed a reputation as something of an eccentric. He taught courses in international politics and advised me to prepare for a career as a political scientist. My background, in his opinion, would equip me ideally for that profession. It would be hard work, he warned, and Gary Cooper, who had indeed attended Grinnell College many years earlier, had dropped out in his freshman year.

I enrolled in Professor Dunner's course and quickly looked to him for friendship and guidance. He was a kind and generous man whose marriage was childless and unhappy. Soon, he began to regard me almost like a son. We would take long walks together in the Iowa countryside. Slowly, I opened up and told him about my boyhood in Europe and in China. He listened with sympathy while drawing on his meerschaum pipe.

I promised him that I would work hard to become a political scientist. I would just as readily have promised him to study astronomy. What I really craved was his affection.

It became my ambition to become the best student in the college and I worked long hours into the night to achieve that goal. Only in that way, I thought, would I be worthy of his love. I drove myself so hard that, one day, my mentor became quite concerned and said: "You are alone too much, and you work too hard. It's spring and I don't think you have even noticed."

Twice a week I abandoned my political science texts for a few hours and walked over to the music building. There, in a small cubicle, I would play snatches of Beethoven sonatas for a while. I went not so much to practice as to give vent to my emotions. While playing, I realized that I wasn't really happy. In fact, I was miserably lonely. Except for Professor Dunner, I hadn't made any friends. The students were cordial and genuinely friendly, but there was no one like Rusty with whom I could share my feelings and develop a sense of emotional intimacy. Rusty and I exchanged long letters, but it was difficult to bridge the distance between two continents. He was studying to be an accountant in Australia. So far as the five hundred girls mentioned by Mrs. Hall were concerned, some were very pretty, even beautiful, but I was much too frightened to approach any of them. It occurred to me that I was almost twenty years old and had never even touched a girl.

One spring evening, I heard a knock on the door of my cubicle.

"Come in," I said. I was playing the slow movement of Beethoven's *Pathétique* Sonata, feeling maudlin and rather sorry for myself. The door opened and a girl walked in. She had dark hair, lively and warm brown eyes, and was wearing a close-fitting sweater.

"You play beautifully," the girl said. I felt myself blushing violently.

"Thank you very much," I managed to stammer in my best British public school English. The girl's eyes lit up.

"Aren't you the foreign student from China?" she asked.

"I have heard about you," she added, laughing. "They call you the Jewish Chinaman."

I looked at her smiling brown eyes and said nothing. I seemed to have lost the power of speech.

"My name is Julie," the girl said and sat down on the chair beside me. "Play some more Beethoven."

I walked her home. At the door, she put her arms around my neck and kissed me on the mouth, pressing her body to mine. I began to tremble. Her mouth was soft and warm. She disengaged herself, and looked at me. Her eyes seemed almost liquid.

"There is a chamber music concert tomorrow night," she said. "I am playing the cello. Why don't you come?"

"Of course I will," I promised.

"You look like an artist," she said. Then she kissed me once more quickly and disappeared.

Julie's home was in a large midwestern city. Her father, she informed me, was a prosperous businessman who had sent her away to college to find a husband. But she preferred artists to businessmen, she said with a laugh, and wasn't ready yet to settle down.

She kissed me again after the concert. This time, she took my hand and placed it gently on her breast. Her heart, I noticed, was racing as wildly as my own. Then she took my head between her hands and looked at me. Her liquid eyes were serious.

"You know, I am a virgin," she said.

"So am I," I blurted out.

Suddenly, we both laughed. Something had happened between us. The awkwardness was gone.

Sunday afternoon, Julie and I rented two bicycles and rode out into the countryside. She had packed a picnic and our destination was a wooded lake area about twenty miles away from the college. Julie wore a light-blue spring dress and looked lovely. We raced part of the way and arrived at the little lake breathless and hungry. The picnic area was crowded with students who had taken advantage of the beautiful spring afternoon to escape from their books. We put on our bathing suits and jumped in the water. Then Julie unpacked the picnic basket and we ate hungrily.

Later, as it began to get dark, I became concerned. I knew that it would take at least an hour to return to school, and I did not want Julie to get into trouble.

"Shouldn't we go back?" I asked.

"Let's stay a while longer," Julie answered. "It's such a beautiful night."

We were lying quietly side by side on our backs. The moon had risen over the lake. The night was very still, and we were completely alone.

Suddenly, Julie sat up and said a little brusquely, "Don't move, I'll be right back."

I continued to lie on my back, looking up into the night sky. But after a while, I became concerned again and sat up. Julie was nowhere to be seen. I rose and walked to the edge of the lake to look out over the water.

It did not take me long to spot Julie. She was swimming in the middle of the lake, her white arms clearly visible in the moonlight. At the shallow end, she stopped swimming, her body rising slowly out of the water. She was completely nude, and looked very beautiful. This is how Adam must have felt when he saw Eve for the first time, I thought to myself. I had lost all fear and walked to the edge of the lake. Julie had come out of the water. Wordlessly, we clung to each other. Love is so simple, I thought. The silkworm moths that I had watched in China flashed through my mind.

"I love you, Julie," I whispered.

"I love you too," she said.

Afterward, we lay together on the grass, holding hands. Neither of us spoke much as we bicycled home. I hated to part from her at the door.

First love. Each time we were together the world was

born again. Julie's love transformed the most ordinary objects around us into something beautiful. Music, pictures, books, all took on a secret meaning. Clichés and banalities were banished; everything was as if for the first time. My life before I had met Julie seemed nothing more than a series of rough, preliminary sketches. I discovered that deep complicity between lovers that excludes everything beyond it. We made the world into our secret garden. Life became a prayer that only Julie's love could grant. When I embraced her, I found a sanctuary beyond the world's perils, a state of grace with pardon granted and justice rendered. For the first time since Rusty and I had had to part, I did not feel alone.

Commencement was only two months away. I was ranked first in my graduating class and had been admitted to graduate school at Harvard with a scholarship. Professor Dunner beamed with pride. I was his best student, he had told me, in many years of teaching. I had good reason to be satisfied with my life, and yet I was not happy. Julie wanted me to marry her and enter her father's business. We had been lovers for more than two years now, and the time had come, she said, to settle down and to have children.

I loved Julie, but the idea of marriage terrified me. Besides, Professor Dunner's encouragement had given me a measure of intellectual self-confidence. I had my heart set on Harvard and wanted to prepare myself for a career in the academic world.

One day in early May, Julie complained of nausea and went to the college infirmary for a checkup. Three days later she appeared at my dormitory white with shock. The college nurse had informed her coldly that she was pregnant and had immediately decided to report her condition to the college dean. An icy terror gripped me. We had been careful, I thought, but obviously not careful enough. I calmed

Julie down as well as I could and went to see my only friend, Professor Dunner.

My mentor heard me out and shook his head. Then he looked at me gravely and said, "You will have to marry her right away and make the best of it."

"What about Harvard?" I asked, and felt my knees going weak under me.

"I don't know," Professor Dunner answered, deep in thought, "we will have to see."

The next morning at ten, I received a call from the office of the college president. I was to see the president at noon. My heart heavy with fear, I walked over to the small administration building. An elderly secretary with bluish hair ushered me in. She was a jolly person who usually had a smile for everyone. Today, she did not smile.

I found myself standing before the president. I did not know Dr. Stevens well. He often preached sermons in Sunday chapel and was known to abhor cigarettes and liquor. Now he looked at me with cold gray eyes, his mouth pressed together in a thin grim line.

"I will ask you only a single question," Dr. Stevens said, pacing up and down before me with his hands folded behind his back. He paused and came to a stop directly in front of me. "Did you have sexual intercourse with Julie?" The question rang out like a pistol shot.

"Yes," I nodded.

"I am sorry to have to tell you this," Dr. Stevens said, "but you are a rotten apple and I have to take measures to make sure that you don't contaminate the other apples in the barrel."

I looked at him. He did not look the least bit sorry for me.

"I am grieved for you, young man," he continued. "Your academic record here has been outstanding; but that is no excuse for flagrant immorality." He took a deep breath. "I have no alternative but to expel you from the college, effective immediately. You will not be permitted to graduate. You are an alien and it is my obligation to report this matter to the immigration authorities. What you and Julie do is your own affair." Dr. Stevens paused, seeming to enjoy the pun. "But you will have to leave the college within the next twenty-four hours. That is all."

He had taken off his glasses and begun to polish them with quick angular movements. His eyes, I noticed, had the look of hard gray marble.

"I offered him my resignation if he does not let you graduate," Dr. Dunner said. It was the next day and I was sitting in the professor's small garden. "That frightened him," he continued. "He has agreed to mail your diploma to you, but you must be gone from here tomorrow. It was the best I could do with that bastard."

I looked at my mentor gratefully. I had never seen him so enraged and noticed with immense relief that his anger was not directed toward me.

"You had better get out of here," Dr. Dunner said gently. "The entire college knows about it." He rose and we shook hands. Then he looked at me and added with a smile, "I don't think Harvard will mind if this earth-shaking scandal should reach Cambridge." As usual, he had read my thoughts.

"Thank you for being a father to me," I said, unable to stop my tears. "I will try to make you proud of me."

"I know you will," Dr. Dunner said.

Julie and I left for St. Louis the next day. Her father welcomed us warmly and did not seem at all perturbed by his daughter's pregnancy. He was a fat little man who liked to smoke large cigars.

"Welcome to the family," he boomed. "I never thought I would have a Jewish Chinaman as a son-in-law. Maybe I'll be blessed with a slant-eyed grandchild." He laughed loudly, savoring his joke.

Julie's mother was in the kitchen trying to feed dozens of relatives who had dropped by to look me over. The wedding date was only a week away. Julie was busy shopping with friends for a wedding gown. In my carpeted guest room, I felt like a prisoner.

A few days later, I received a call from the local office of the Immigration and Naturalization Service. An inspector wished to see me immediately.

"We have had a complaint against you on grounds of moral turpitude," the immigration official began. He seemed embarrassed and kept scratching his crew cut. "We may have to begin deportation proceedings against you." A nameless terror rose in my throat.

"Where to?" I managed to croak.

"What was your place of residence before you entered the United States?" the inspector asked in a businesslike tone.

"Shanghai, China."

"Well, we can't very well ship you back there," the inspector said after a moment's hesitation. "The commies have taken over there, haven't they?" I nodded. Mao Tsetung's army had occupied Shanghai six months ago. "I guess we will have to deport you to your place of origin. Where were you born?" he suddenly asked.

"Vienna, Austria," I said.

The inspector began to scratch his head again.

"Haven't the commies taken over that town too?" he wanted to know.

"Vienna is divided into four sectors," I replied dutifully, "and one of them is occupied by the Soviet Union."

"And in which sector were you born?" the inspector asked. His voice had become impatient. I hesitated. I had no idea in which of the four sectors the little house of my birth was located. It was probably a heap of rubble by now anyway.

"In the Russian sector," I said.

"Damn!" The inspector had leaned back in his armchair and was looking at me. I seemed to be causing endless trouble for him. "We can't ship you back into the arms of our enemies after we have paid for your education," he said, scratching his head again. "What the hell is your nationality?" he asked suddenly, his face brightening.

"I have no nationality," I answered truthfully. "The Germans made me into a stateless refugee." The inspector glared at me. His face had become angry. But then he suddenly began to laugh. He laughed so loud that he was bellowing.

"Pete," he yelled to a man sitting behind a desk a few feet away. "I don't know what to do with this guy; he is the original man without a country. We may have to invent a country to deport him to."

Pete shuffled over. He was an older man with a balding head. "Aren't you supposed to be marrying an American citizen?" Pete asked.

"Yes," I answered, "the day after tomorrow."

"You had better do it fast," Pete said. Then he turned to the crew cut. "Let him go, Mike," he said. "The boy is about to become a father." Pete winked at me and handed me a cigar. I took it and put it in my pocket.

"Thank you, sir," I said. "Thank you very much."

"You've got a week," said Pete. Mike scratched his head, saying nothing. He was still scratching when I walked out the door.

The wedding was a large and noisy affair. I went through it like a stone. In a haze, I listened to a rabbi pronounce the marriage vows and heard myself say, "I do." Then dozens of people I had never seen slapped me on the back and stuffed money into my pockets. I fished out the bills and gave them all to Julie. She looked radiant, but I looked at her as if she were a stranger. I knew she loved me but all I felt was guilt and terror. What I had loved was the romantic girl who had walked toward me out of the lake in the woods. What I saw before me now was a full-grown woman, eager to take on the duties of a wife and mother. But I was still a boy, it seemed, though a boy about to become a father.

A heavy hand slapped me on the back. It was Julie's father. He was slightly drunk and out of breath. He and Julie had been dancing. He was patting his daughter's belly. "She dances pretty good, the little mother," he said proudly. Then he turned to me and said, "Son, tomorrow morning you come with me to the office. I want to break you in as a future partner. And here is my wedding gift to you—it's a dowry, just like in the old country." He stuffed a piece of paper into my pocket. Julie smiled at her father, her eyes dancing.

"Thank you, Daddy," she said, kissing him on the cheek.

"Thank you, sir," I mumbled. I took the piece of paper out of my pocket. It was a check for ten thousand dollars, made out in my name.

"From now on you will call me Dad," said Julie's father.

On our wedding night Julie wanted to make love, but my body refused to cooperate. At least that part of me is honest, I thought in self-disgust. I was afraid of Julie, afraid to tell her the truth that I did not want to be a partner in her father's business, that instead I yearned to go to Harvard with my scholarship.

"We will have a good life," Julie said lovingly. "I hope we will have a son."

I said nothing. All I felt was terrible guilt. I didn't want to be a husband and I didn't want a child. I had agreed to marry Julie because I had no choice. Suddenly I was gripped with a violent urge to kill myself, to slash my wrists, my throat, anything to stop this guilt, this pain. The memory of Papa flooded through me. Perhaps suicide was easy for those who have it in the family, I thought. It seemed like a natural thing to do, almost like walking from one room to another, far from the complex theories I had read about in a psychology text at school. Despair, self-hatred, and hopelessness, I thought, were quite enough. I was a child of suicide: I would kill myself and join Papa. At last, I thought, the dream would have a happy ending. I would see his face again. I got out of bed, put on my clothes, and left the house. Julie had fallen asleep.

I walked along the banks of the Mississippi River looking for a place to jump. Twice I took a running leap and stopped just in time. Despite my despair, I was beginning to feel ridiculous. I suspected that, even if I jumped, I would probably try to swim to safety. Instead of yet another try, I reached into my pocket to blow my nose, and felt a piece of paper. It was the check for ten thousand dollars made out to me by Julie's father. I looked at it for a long time, then slowly tore it into several small pieces which I threw into the water. Dawn was breaking when I returned to the house.

Julie was awake when I walked in. She was frantic with worry. We were to leave for a one-month honeymoon that afternoon.

"Where on earth have you been?" she asked, her eyes searching mine.

"Please sit down," I said. My voice must have carried a new authority. She obeyed without a word.

"Julie," I said, "I will not be a partner in your father's business. I have torn up the check and thrown it into the Mississippi. I will go to Harvard. If you come with me, I will do my best to make our marriage work, but if you don't, I will go alone."

Julie's eyes became dark. For a long time, she said nothing.

"I will go alone, then," I repeated.

"You are crazy, completely mad," she said.

"Look here," I implored, reaching for her hand, "if I am unhappy, I shall make you and the child unhappy too." Julie had begun to cry.

"You are throwing away your life," she sobbed. "Here you have a family, I love you as I will never love another man and Dad already looks at you as if you were his son. He always wanted a son," she sobbed hysterically. "Someday you will take over his business. What is it that you want that we can't give you?"

"I don't want to be a businessman," I answered miserably.

"Go to your damn Harvard then," Julie screamed suddenly at the top of her voice. Her eyes had become wild with despair. "I thought you loved me!"

"I did," I answered truthfully.

"And now?" Julie looked at me, her liquid eyes imploring me.

"Of course I love you," I lied, reaching for her hand.

We made love awkwardly, almost like two strangers. How can feelings shift so quickly, I thought to myself. Two hours ago I was close to suicide and now I was enjoying sex with my bride. It occurred to me that if sex could make me feel that much better, I was certainly not ready to kill myself. Or perhaps I was enjoying it because I had dared to be more honest. I didn't really know. Later, we fell asleep in each other's arms.

Toward noon, there was a knock at our bedroom door. It was Julie's father.

"Time to show you the business," he said through the door. "I have changed your tickets so that you can leave on your honeymoon tomorrow."

"Thank you, sir," I said, "but I am not going."

"Okay, take your time," Julie's father replied. I heard him laugh as he went down the stairs.

I looked at Julie.

"Are you still going?" she asked.

"Yes," I said. Nothing had changed. Julie watched in silence as I packed my few belongings.

"You really are crazy," she repeated. It was like a rerun of the earlier scene.

"I probably am," I said. Suddenly, I felt a surge of strength course through my body. For the first time in my life I no longer felt quite so helpless. The guilt was still there but it was no longer crushing me. "Goodbye," I said. Julie jumped out of bed and ran toward me.

"I will be waiting for you here when you come to your senses," she whispered softly, putting her arms around me.

"I will not come to my senses," I replied. Then I walked out the door, and crept noiselessly past the living room. I was afraid to run into Julie's father. I am still a goddamn coward, I said to myself. But maybe I can learn. Then I made my way to the bus terminal. Three hours later, I was on a Greyhound bus heading east for Boston.

I gazed out the window at the flatlands rushing by. A heavy sadness weighed upon me. If Julie had stood by me against her parents' will, if she had affirmed me in my wish to learn and grow, our love might have endured. Together, we might have overcome the trauma of the shotgun marriage. If only she had come with me to Harvard or even spontaneously offered to, all might have been well. Now it would never be the same. Love dies, I thought, when lovers fashion cages for each other. The bars are their own needs. I was alone again. Perhaps we survive, I thought, not only by what we learn, but also by what we manage to forget.

Chapter Five

I took a ten-dollar bill out of my pocket and handed it to Mrs. Hersey. The old landlady slowly climbed the stairs of the little wooden house all the way up to the attic.

"This room is ten dollars a week," she said, "two weeks' rent in advance."

"Fine," I said, and gave her another ten-dollar bill.

"The bathroom is one flight below," Mrs. Hersey added, "and there is a pay telephone on the street corner." She folded the two bills carefully and wrote out a receipt. "Do you have any more luggage?" she asked. I shook my head.

"That's it," I answered, pointing to the two bags I had carried up the stairs. Mrs. Hersey hesitated a moment.

"There is a laundry two blocks away," she said. "They give you one-day service there." Then she shuffled out and closed the door.

The room was hot and stuffy. I opened the window and looked out on a row of wooden houses. The sight was depressing and I decided to take a walk and think over my situation. I had arrived in Cambridge the night before with less than fifty dollars to my name. It was late June and it would be three more months before the fall semester was to begin. I had been so eager to get to Harvard that I had arrived almost three months early. Now, I had no place else to go and was practically broke. I would have to find a job not only to last the summer but to save some money for September. The scholarship money wouldn't be enough for room and board during the academic year.

A young boy near Harvard Square was selling newspapers and seemed to be doing a brisk business. I bought a paper and looked at the headline: "Aggression in Korea," it proclaimed in bold red ink. There was no end to it, I thought as I walked through Harvard Yard. Only five years after Hiroshima, young men would again be dying. I felt a surge of helplessness and rage. Perhaps I should not have torn up that check after all. Perhaps Julie's father had been right. "Look after your wife and kid," he had said, "and let the rest of the world go to hell." I thought of Julie and missed her soft warm body. Maybe she too had been right, I thought, maybe I really was crazy.

I stopped in front of a small luncheonette with a "Counterman Wanted" sign in the window. Why not? I thought, opened the door, and sat down at the counter. A little man with a handlebar mustache and jet-black hair darted back and forth behind the counter. "One cheeseburger, heavy on the french fries," he yelled into the kitchen. "Come on, Charlie, I ordered that burger ten minutes ago," grunted a man with enormous buttocks that were spilling down over the counter stool.

"What will it be?" Charlie was wiping off the counter in front of me.

"I want the job," I replied. Charlie stopped wiping and looked up.

"Forty bucks a week plus tips and lunch," he said, "eight hours a day. You can start right now."

"Okay," I said, "give me an apron."

I lasted at Charlie's less than two weeks. The work was hard and tips were meager. After lunch, when the rush was over, Charlie made us wash the dishes and clean the floor. For lunch, he permitted only spaghetti and two meatballs. Absalom, the black cook, began to feel sorry for me and regularly hid two more meatballs under the spaghetti. Thus, every day at three o'clock, I carried a mountain of spaghetti topped with the two visible meatballs past Charlie's watchful eye. On one occasion, for some unknown reason, Charlie became suspicious.

"Hold it," he commanded suddenly, as I was carrying my lunch plate to the far end of the counter. He took a fork and poked around in the spaghetti. It did not take long to discover the contraband at the bottom of the plate. Charlie looked at me and made a lightning calculation.

"Two extra meatballs at a quarter apiece for ten days makes five dollars even," he said quietly, holding out his hand.

I reached into my pocket and handed him a five-dollar bill. Taking off my apron, I thought desperately of some particularly brilliant parting insult to throw in his face. None occurred to me. Absalom had come out of the kitchen and was grinning behind Charlie's back. He held up two fingers in a victory sign. He must have been a soldier in the war, I thought, as I closed the door behind me.

I made my way to the headquarters of the Check Protection Corporation in downtown Boston. Charlie's pride had been a check-writing machine that he had installed next to the cash register. The machine imprinted each check with Charlie's name and perforated the amounts for which the checks were written. "Protects me against forgery," Charlie had declared proudly.

One afternoon, a salesman had come in to service the machine. He had left me his card.

"There is good money to be made with these machines," he said. "Each sale means a profit of a hundred dollars. When you get tired of this dumb job, come and see us."

"It's hard work," said Steve, the chief of the firm's sales

force. He had explained the basic pitch to me. It consisted of going from door to door with a sample machine, demonstrating its virtues and appealing to the prospective buyer's ego and his fear. The personal nameplate was for the ego and the perforator for the fear. The top salesmen pitched about thirty businesses a day and averaged about ten sales a week. Each sale meant a net profit of eighty dollars. If I could sell one machine a day for the rest of the summer, I calculated, the profits would see me through the first year of graduate school.

After a week's apprenticeship, I was ready, and walked into the office of a lobster retailer on the south Boston wharf.

"Sir," I said tentatively to the owner, "have you heard that there have been a lot of check forgeries lately in this neighborhood?" The man looked up. He was wearing rubber gloves and sorting lobsters.

"No," he said, "I haven't."

"Sir," I continued in a businesslike tone, "do you mail your checks?"

"Sure," the businessman replied, "that's normal business procedure, isn't it?"

"Let me show you what risks you run," I said gravely, pulling out a recent issue of the Boston *Globe*. On the front page were two men in handcuffs who had been arrested for check forgery.

"Do you know what these men did?" I asked. The man shook his head. He had taken off his rubber gloves. I took a specimen check out of my pocket.

"Write down your signature," I said. The man looked up hesitantly.

"Don't worry, I will tear it up in a minute," I promised. "Now give me one of your business envelopes." He handed me an envelope.

"Now please put the signed check into the envelope and seal it," I requested. The man obeyed and licked the envelope.

"Now watch me," I said.

I took out a pair of knitting needles and inserted them into the air hole of the envelope. Grasping the check between the needles, I rolled it up inside the sealed envelope and slowly pulled it out through the air hole.

"By the way, may I have your name, sir?" I said politely.

"Fish," said the man. I looked at him incredulously.

"That's right, Barrington Fish," he repeated.

"Now watch me copy your signature," I continued. I had learned that almost any signature could be reproduced by placing the original upside down and copying it backward. I managed a fair facsimile of Mr. Fish's signature. By now I had his rapt attention.

"They get ahold of your mail," I said, "then they extract the check and study your signature. They put the check back in and it reaches its proper destination. But two or three weeks later, they cash checks with your signature, and by the time you find out about it, they are gone and you are out a lot of money." I stopped a moment and took out the sample check writer.

"How much is this goddamn thing?" asked Mr. Fish.

"One hundred fifty dollars," I replied.

"I'll take it," said the lobsterman. "I will write you the check on the machine."

We concluded the transaction and shook hands. I had earned eighty dollars in less than twenty minutes.

During the next two months, I sold an average of one machine a day. Steve had been right. It was grueling work and most of the time I did not get much past the door. One afternoon, I decided to ring the bell of a funeral parlor. A pale-faced man with slicked-down hair led me to an adjacent ice-cold room smelling of formaldehyde.

"Mr. Santori," said the man to a figure bent over a large table, "a salesman here to see you."

"Well?" asked Santori impatiently. I noticed that he was injecting fluid into what appeared to be a corpse. "I am embalming this man," Santori said, noticing my look. "If you want to sell me something, you will have to watch." Halfway through my pitch, Santori waved his hand and interrupted: "I don't write any checks," he declared imperiously, "all my business is done in cash."

"You mean you send cash through the mails?" I asked, making a last effort.

"No," Santori replied, "I don't use the mails either."

"No checks, no mail?" I said, my courage fading fast.

"That's right," Santori said, "I don't trust banks, I don't trust the mail; and I certainly don't trust you." He had finished his embalming work and was slowly coming toward me.

"I am sorry," I said quickly, backing out the door. "I am sorry to have bothered you."

By Labor Day, I had saved up almost three thousand dollars. Students were beginning to come into town and filled up the rooming houses near the university. I discovered that my diploma from Grinnell had been received in good order. Professor Dunner had kept his word. I had not had word from Julie, but had learned that Oscar and my mother had fled China and were settled in New York. When I went to register for classes, the dean congratulated me on my scholarship.

"You did a great job out there at Grinnell," he said. "We are happy to have you here at Harvard." Then he held out his hand to me and smiled.

My fellow students whom I met at mealtimes during the next few days were a small but formidable group. One was a brilliant Polish Catholic who was engrossed in Stalin's bloody purges. Zbigniew Brzezinski had a quick and powerful intelligence with a touch of playful cruelty toward those who were not armed with his extraordinary gift for repartee. A conversation with him tended to resemble a barrage of staccatolike artillery fire. An impish face beneath a shock of unruly blond hair gave "Zbig" the appearance of a high school boy. But it was very seldom that I saw anyone get the better of him.

Austrian-born but Sorbonne-educated, and an intellectual through and through, Stanley Hoffmann was endowed with a charming Gallic wit which masked a basic shyness and carefully guarded sense of privacy.

George Liska, who had fled from the Communists in Prague, cut an elegant but remote figure which reminded me of a medieval cardinal. Kafka-like and melancholy, he often spoke in riddles and tended toward solitude. Samuel Huntington, a native-born American, was studying the relationship between the soldier and the state. To the amazement of most of us, he suggested that America had more to learn from West Point than West Point from America.

All of us believed that the atomic bomb had changed our world forever. Most of us looked at the study of history with impatience and suspicion. The past could not help us much, we thought.

There was one anomaly in our midst. We had heard that a senior at Harvard College had submitted a 377-page undergraduate honors thesis, modestly entitled "The Meaning of History." Rumor had it that Professor William Elliott had read the first one hundred pages and awarded the young senior a summa cum laude. This aroused our interest and envy for several reasons. In the first place, a summa cum laude was extremely rare and exempted the fortunate recipient from the dreaded oral examination for the doctorate; second, we were struck by the content of the thesis: this undergraduate had dared to take on Spengler, Toynbee, and Kant; and finally, and most incomprehensibly, this bachelor of arts had apparently announced his intention to write a doctoral thesis for the department of government on the diplomacy of the early nineteenth century. Our curiosity was aroused even further since none of us had ever met the author of "The Meaning of History." The young man had a reputation for brooding in the stacks of Widener Library while we were discussing the latest events on the world scene. But one day, in early October 1950, he joined us at our luncheon table. That was when I first met Henry Kissinger.

Kissinger was several years older than most of us and seemed austere and rather distant. His close-cropped hair gave him a stern and military look. I had heard that he was a Jewish refugee from Germany and that he had served as a sergeant in the military occupation of his homeland. Inevitably, the conversation drifted to the subject of his dissertation. He was interested in the problem of peace, Kissinger explained. The Congress of Vienna of 1815 had attracted his attention. The challenges of those distant days struck him as analogous to those of our time. We were astounded. Had he not heard of the atom bomb? someone asked. What could Metternich and Castlereagh possibly teach us? Brzezinski smiled and suggested that Henry might wish to transfer to the history department. Kissinger, totally unruffled, rose from the table and got himself another helping of chicken à la king.

What impressed me most about Henry Kissinger during that luncheon discussion was his self-assurance and intellectual power. He argued forcefully and brilliantly. It did not seem to me, however, as I listened, that Henry was particularly interested in impressing or converting anyone around him. It seemed almost as if he were carrying on a dialogue with himself rather than with his interlocutors. We did not quite know what to make of him. There was something puzzling about him. And one also sensed a fierce ambition.

When he had completed his exposition, Kissinger left the table. The rest of us immediately began to discuss his thesis. Someone asked under which professor Kissinger was planning to work. It turned out that William Elliott had agreed to continue as his mentor. Elliott was one of the two most powerful professors in the government department. The other was Carl J. Friedrich. Both men taught political philosophy and were bitter intellectual rivals. Any doctoral student found out soon after his arrival that he had to make a choice between Elliott and Friedrich. It apparently was impossible to be on cordial terms with both. Perhaps the most remarkable thing about Henry Kissinger, most of us thought, was the fact that he had managed to be on excellent terms with both these supreme rivals of the Harvard government department. Not without envy, I wondered how he managed that. No one knew the answer.

Henry Kissinger and his wife Anne lived in a small apartment near the university. Anne was a shy, attractive girl who, like her husband, had fled from Nazi Germany. She seemed to be content to live in Henry's shadow and seldom spoke much in his presence. Once, when I rang their doorbell on a Sunday afternoon, Anne opened the door and put her finger to her mouth.

"Talk softly," she said, "Henry is thinking."

After a while, Henry emerged from his study, still deep in thought.

"Castlereagh's suicide was a tragedy for Metternich," he said to no one in particular, taking off his glasses. "Metternich lost his one dependable friend."

I nodded. I didn't really know much about Metternich, but I admired Henry's single-minded dedication to his work, even though it frightened me a little. It was always the same with him. Whatever preoccupied him at the moment would become the subject of our conversation. I quickly recognized that Henry's ambitions ranged far beyond the academic world and that he would let nothing stop him. On one occasion, I told him about my problems with Julie.

"Don't waste your energy on silly little girls," he said curtly.

I looked at him in consternation, but he had not meant to be cruel or unkind. He had simply stated his priorities. There was about Henry a sense of brooding melancholy. The past somehow always hovered over him. I knew, of course, about his youth as a Jew in Nazi Germany and his escape, barely in time, from the coming Holocaust. He knew my similar history, but we seldom talked about it, partially out of fear of causing the other anguish with painful memories, but also because Henry tended to withdraw when the conversation became personal.

"The past is dead," he told me once, "I am interested in the future." I was deeply drawn to him and he, too, sought me out.

"You are a good friend," he would often say to me. And yet, when I would try to talk about emotions rather than about intellectual or professional pursuits, the barriers went up. In the end, although I recognized his genius, I sometimes felt lonely in his presence.

If Henry had an intellectual mentor, it was another Jewish refugee from Germany. Professor Hans J. Morgenthau, almost a generation older than most of us, had just published a major work in world politics which was to become the leading classic in the field. Not surprisingly, Morgenthau's vision of the world was a tragic one. It rejected the facile belief in progress and the rationality of man that had been typical of most American thinkers. Instead, he advanced a "realist theory" which regarded the struggle for power as the essence of international relations everywhere and always. Morgenthau taught a seminar at Harvard as a visiting professor and most of us attended. I, too, was attracted by his uncompromising honesty and intellectual daring. His deeply pessimistic lectures were laced with a brilliant, mordant wit that was very similar to Henry's own. On one occasion, an eager, somewhat unsophisticated student wanted to know whether the United Nations was being faithful to the ideals of its charter. "The count of Hesse-Coburg was once asked whether he had been faithful to his wife," Morgenthau replied, "and he answered, 'Sometimes.'"

Across the hallway from the Kissingers lived my mentor, Inis Claude, and his wife, Marie. I had been too timid to approach either Elliott or Friedrich and had instead befriended this young instructor who taught a course on the United Nations. Claude was a first-rate lecturer and quickly managed to arouse my interest in the new world organization. Soon he made me his assistant and suggested that I write a doctoral thesis on the world refugee problem. Over dinner at his home, Claude would be a kind and gentle critic of my work while Marie would listen quietly, sewing a woolen shirt for me.

Sometimes Henry would drop by and the conversation would shift abruptly from refugees and the United Nations to the theories of Oswald Spengler. On one such occasion, another young instructor who was a dinner guest tried to steer the conversation to academic politics. Henry glared at him.

"You are wasting energy," he declared contemptuously. "The fights among academics are so dirty because the stakes are so low." The young instructor fell silent and left shortly afterward, hardly able to conceal his rage. Henry seemed quite unaware that he had insulted the young man. He had simply decided that the conversation was a waste of time.

"Everyone should read Spengler," Henry said, returning to his favorite topic. "The president could benefit from reading him. I think I shall bring *The Decline of the West* to his attention." Inis Claude and I exchanged a glance. Henry was cleaning his eyeglasses, deep in thought. "Yes, I think I will send it to the president," he muttered to himself with a small smile.

When I returned home that evening, a letter was waiting for me. It was from Julie. "We have a son," she wrote. "I am ready to try and live with you in Cambridge." There was a P.S. below her signature. "We will have to live on your income," it said. "Daddy never wants to talk to you again."

"May I have another piece of chicken?" I asked Julie. We were having dinner in the kitchenette of our two-room flat. The baby had finally stopped crying and was sleeping in his crib. Julie shook her head.

"I only bought two chicken legs," she said. "I was short of cash again."

I looked into the empty pot and then at Julie. This can't go on, I thought in silent desperation. Ever since Julie had joined me in Cambridge a year ago and I had to support her and the child, my studies had suffered grievously. I was again selling check writers, and on weekends, I helped a local rabbi with his correspondence. Afternoons were taken up with seminars. This left evenings and nights for work on my dissertation which had to be defended before the end of the semester. I was totally exhausted. Yet sleep was a major luxury since the baby cried incessantly. There was neither time nor privacy for anything. My first romance had turned into a sour marriage.

"Julie," I said quietly one evening, "I think you had better go home or we will either kill each other or go crazy."

Julie looked at me with her liquid eyes which were still beautiful. "Make love to me," she said simply.

Surprised, I looked at her. Suddenly a great wave of tenderness came over me. I led her to our little bed and there we loved each other silently so as not to wake the little boy. When it was over, we both cried. Then we fell asleep, holding on to one another.

The next morning, I left early with my sample case and Julie kissed me goodbye at the door. I sold a machine to the owner of a filling station and bought a pint of ice cream on the way home. When I entered the little flat, Julie was nowhere to be seen and the crib was empty. Then I saw the note on the kitchen table. "I am leaving while we still love each other," it said. "If you want to contact me, I will be with Daddy."

I sat down at the kitchen table numb with shock. I had begun to be attached to my little son. For a long time I stared at the empty crib. Then it occurred to me that Julie had been right to leave. I probably would not have had the courage to leave a second time. As I sat there, I thought of the girl whom I had loved long ago in the summer silence. I sat for a very long time, frozen, waiting for the pain. Then I ate the ice cream.

About fifty students were sitting around the little foyer in Memorial Hall. Some had taken out their textbooks and had begun to read. Others were chatting or fidgeting impatiently on their chairs. One couple had retired into a corner near the fireplace and the boy was kissing his girl's ear. It was past nine o'clock and we had been waiting for over half an hour for the appearance of the little-known Welsh poet who was to give a reading from his latest verses.

In no mood to work on my dissertation, I had taken the evening off. Ever since Julie had left six months earlier, I had been working at a furious pace. In my spare time, I sold machines in order to send Julie money for the support of our son. But tonight I was exhausted. Besides, I rationalized, Friday night was not a good time to sell people check-writing machines. I loved Dylan Thomas's poetry and had come early to get a good seat near the front. It had not been difficult since the room was far from crowded. But now I was beginning to get anxious. Perhaps the poet would not appear at all. It was known that he had cancelled many times without apparent reason.

Suddenly, I heard the shuffling of feet outside the door. Three men walked in side by side, pressed very close together. Two of them were wearing impeccably pressed clothes, striped ties, and button-down shirts. The well-groomed men were holding up the third between them, whom I recognized instantly as Dylan Thomas. The poet wore a rumpled suit that hung on him like a potato sack. Holding on to the arms of the two young deans, he walked unsteadily to the rostrum. "He is drunk," I heard a student say in an audible whisper. A slight titter ran through the waiting crowd as the poet fumbled in his pockets and clumsily took out some notes. Then he waited silently for the commotion to subside. My God, I thought, my romantic image crumbling, he looks exactly like a tired salesman.

Dylan Thomas gazed at us with a look that struck me as reproachful. You know who I am, it seemed to say, so why do you humiliate me? Then he bent his tousled head over his notes and began to read. At once the room fell absolutely silent. I realized again that imprisoned in this shapeless body dwelt the spirit of poetic genius. His rich sonorous voice enveloped us in cadences that sounded more like music than the spoken word. The sheer beauty of the verses brought me close to tears. Time seemed suspended. "And you, my father, there on that sad height," the poet read, "do not go gentle into that good night; Rage, rage against the dying of the light.

"Thank you," Dylan Thomas said after a pause and stuffed his notes back into his pockets.

There was a loud and sustained round of applause. The poet smiled for the first time and his face suddenly appeared almost boyish. Then he stepped away from the lectern that had seemed much too high for him and walked quickly to the door. His step was firm now and there was no trace of unsteadiness. At the door he smiled again and waved his arm in a gesture of farewell. The applause seemed to have buoyed his spirits. Two minutes later he was gone.

I glanced across the aisle. A girl was weeping convulsively, her entire body wracked with sobs. A few of the students who had stayed behind were looking at her in embarrassment. Following an instinct, I walked across the aisle and touched the girl's shoulder.

"May I help you?" I heard myself say.

The girl glanced at me. Then her hand shot up as if to ward off a blow. I looked into a pair of large dark eyes set in an expressive face of haunting beauty. The blackness of her eyes and hair highlighted the white translucence of her skin. With her hand up, as if in self-defense, the girl seemed fragile and infinitely vulnerable. Losing my own timidity, I helped her gently from her seat.

"Thank you," she whispered, taking my arm tentatively. "I think he will die soon," I heard her say softly to herself.

During the next few months, I saw a lot of Wanda and fell hopelessly in love with her. She was a student who had been in and out of mental institutions several times. The doctors, Wanda told me, were of the opinion that as a result of massive deprivation in her early years, she had lived a life of fantasy and had made a poor adjustment to reality. Wanda disagreed with the doctors' diagnosis. She believed with absolute conviction that the world was insane and that adaptation to it was the ultimate capitulation. Happiness in such a world was just a lot of Communist propaganda. The sanatorium, she said on one occasion, was the last refuge of sanity in a satanic world.

The intensity of my feelings for Wanda frightened me. It was like an insatiable hunger that was growing deep inside me. Lovemaking, I noticed to my own amazement, did little to satisfy that hunger. Though Wanda was passionate, I sensed an emotional barrier that I was unable to penetrate. It seemed that she almost had to keep me at a distance in order to be able to make love.

My repeated efforts to break down her resistance and to achieve a sense of intimacy were met with flashes of sudden anger or with sullen opposition. Once, we lay in bed exhausted and I began to talk to her. I had been trying for weeks to tell her about my past in Europe and in China, but she had always changed the subject. We were holding hands.

"You know, my father killed himself in Europe," I suddenly blurted out, for no apparent reason.

Wanda withdrew her hand and sat up in bed. I noticed that her face had become contorted with rage. Suddenly, she lunged at me and hit me in the face, again and again.

"I don't want to hear about it," she shrieked, as she pummelled me with her small fists. Finally, she stopped and I held her in my arms. She had begun to cry hysterically.

"Hit me," she suddenly said between sobs. I did not respond. "Hit me," she repeated, her voice rising.

"Wanda," I said as gently as I could, "why can't we ever talk about ourselves to one another?"

"I don't know," Wanda answered hopelessly. The storm had passed and she had stopped crying.

Even though Wanda became more and more withdrawn, I was unable to leave her. In fact, the more she pulled away from me emotionally, the greater became my need for intimacy. It was as if she were a mirror of my own loneliness, as if through healing her, I might be able to heal myself. Despite the fact that I knew very little about her past, I felt a sense of recognition, a kind of common tragedy that, while not to be discussed in words, nevertheless forged a common bond. Sex between us was a kind of affirmation, a respite from despair. Side by side, but not together, we would race toward that transient consummation that always left us even lonelier than before.

One day Wanda did not show up for an appointment for a concert in Memorial Hall. Concerned, I ran all the way to Radcliffe, where I was informed that Wanda had been taken to a mental institution fifty miles away. She had had another breakdown. Wracked with anxiety and guilt, I drove out to the hospital and asked to see her doctor.

"We know about you," the psychiatrist said, motioning me to take a chair. "We had hoped that you might be good for her, but she has had a relapse. It's not your fault. You should know that her condition is grave and the reasons for it go back a very long time."

"Can you tell me about her?" I asked. I noticed that my hands were trembling as I drank the tea which a nurse had poured for me.

Wanda's stepfather, I discovered, had seduced his daughter when she was thirteen. Her mother, unable to prevent this horror, had been so consumed by guilt that she committed suicide shortly afterward. The man then forced the teenage girl into an affair that lasted for two years, until Wanda went away to college.

"You are the first normal relationship she has had," the doctor told me. "I hope that you can come to see her often."

"How long will she have to stay here?" I asked. The doctor shook his head.

"There is no way of telling," he replied. "At least a year or two, I think."

I visited Wanda at the hospital every other Sunday. We would take long walks on the hospital grounds and sometimes a nurse gave us a box lunch. The doctor had warned that I should not be drawn into Wanda's world of fantasy, but that I should attempt to assist in her gradual adjustment to reality. What happened, however, was virtually the opposite. If Wanda was insane, her madness had a profound logic and lucidity that gradually began to draw me in. On one occasion, I had brought a textbook with me. Wanda picked it up and pointed to a passage that described the problem of nuclear deterrence. "The safety of people," the passage read, "depends upon the safety of weapons. If both the United States and the Soviet Union are assured that they are able mutually to destroy each other, they will be deterred from doing so."

"Mutually assured destruction," Wanda said, "that spells mad."

"That's right," I admitted, surprised.

"It wouldn't shock me," Wanda said, "if the people who write this stuff are a lot crazier than I am. The patients here are harmless. All they do is walk in the sun and sometimes they take off their clothes and dance in the grass. But they don't go around killing one another."

I looked at her and felt a surge of love well up within me. She was right, I thought. Perhaps her sickness was a form of courage and my sanity was weakness.

"I am inventing a new language," Wanda said, "a language that will bring more beauty into the world. Would you like to learn it?"

I thought of what the doctor had said and shook my head. Wanda looked at me in silence.

"You know, madness may be a rational decision," she said quietly, "but it takes courage to make the leap because one may not wish ever to return."

She had read my thoughts. "No, Wanda," I said.

"Then leave me," Wanda shrieked suddenly, her eyes burning with anger. "Everybody always does."

Her outburst had attracted a nurse, who quickly led Wanda away. I gazed after her small frail figure till she had disappeared into the building. Then I walked to my car and drove back to Cambridge.

Two months later I received my doctorate. Commencement was a lonely business. After the ceremony, I looked at my diploma. "Doctor of Philosophy," it said. I thought of Wanda and the courage of her broken heart. Courage, it occurred to me, was a rarer gift than brains. I was adapting to the world. I knew that I would not see Wanda again. The pull of her abyss was powerful and she might yet drag me into it with her. The price of her love, I suddenly realized, was madness.

Inis Claude walked over from the academic procession and warmly shook my hand. There was a teaching job open in New York, he said. Was I interested?

"Yes," I said, without a moment's hesitation. Claude looked at me, surprised.

"You should think it over for a week," he admonished gently.

"You are right," I answered gratefully.

Cambridge without Wanda had become empty and oppressive and I felt I had to leave. With some amazement it occurred to me that the choice of my profession had little, if anything, to do with reason. My driving need for a kind and loving father had determined the choice for me. Perhaps, I thought, only a thin barrier separated me from Wanda. Perhaps her madness was merely loneliness stemming from her heart's refusal to engage in compromise. Somehow I felt that I had compromised. I was going to be someone I was not. For a moment, I felt a desperate urge to speak to Wanda and to ask for her advice. But then it struck me as absurd to ask a mental patient for advice about my future. And so, two days later, I took the train to New York City.

Chapter Six

I walked out on the stage of the large rotunda of Columbia University in my new tuxedo. Dr. Grayson Kirk, the president, was waiting for me at the rostrum. He held a plaque in one hand and an envelope in the other.

"We are proud to honor you today," he said to me, "for having written *The Might of Nations,* the finest book on international relations published in the year 1962." Dr. Kirk handed me the plaque and warmly shook my hand. "The Bancroft Prize is one of the most generous awards in the academic world," he declared, facing the audience. "It carries an award of four thousand dollars." He smiled and handed me the envelope. I looked out over the five hundred elegant applauding people who had braved an April rainstorm to come out and honor me.

"Thank you, Mr. President," I managed to say. My voice, I knew, was none too steady. I had decided to make my acceptance speech as short as possible. The reason was that I felt like an impostor or, even worse, a fraud.

In 1963, I was thirty-six, a tenured full professor at a leading liberal arts college in New York City. I was a popular teacher and enjoyed a solid reputation as a scholar. In addition, I was in wide demand as a lecturer all over the United

States. My relations with my colleagues at the college were generally good. My income was more than sufficient to meet my needs since Julie had married a wealthy St. Louis pharmacist. I had rented a spacious bachelor apartment on Central Park overlooking the reservoir and had even bought a grand piano. Oscar had died of a malignancy on his adrenal gland the year before and my mother, secretly relieved to be rid of him, had opened a tiny millinery store on upper Broadway. My health was excellent and I enjoyed regular tennis at a private club within walking distance of my home. On weekends, I generally drove my new convertible into the countryside. To all appearances, I was a happy and successful man. The truth was that I felt bored and miserable.

I had climbed the rungs of the academic ladder with unusual speed and realized, not without anxiety, that there were no more promotions to be had. From now on, I would have to set my own standards for my work. Any satisfaction would have to flow from its inherent value rather than from a committee of professors passing judgment on my tenure or promotion. I had just published a prize-winning book and the thought of beginning the agonizing chore of writing another frightened me. Not yet forty, I had reached a professional plateau with few summits left to climb. The thought of teaching the same college courses for the next twenty or thirty years made me uneasy. There seemed to be nowhere else to go.

My relationships with women in those years were superficial at best. Since I had learned that Wanda had committed suicide shortly after her release from the hospital I had resisted any deep emotional involvement. A procession of women had passed through my life without touching me at all. It was as if something in me had gone numb. Enviously, I watched my colleagues marry and have children as I carried on my multiple, often simultaneous, affairs. Frequently, I led a double or even triple life. The lies and deceptions that were the necessary consequence angered and exhausted me. Yet my fear of loneliness was so intense that I was seldom able to break off a relationship. Usually, a woman would abandon me when she realized at last that I would not marry her. Each separation then was like an echo of some distant pain. Yet, it was preferable to the prospect of a mediocre marriage.

One such separation caused me considerable anguish. I had become involved with the daughter of a professor whom I admired greatly. Eva had fallen in love with me and wanted us to marry, but I perceived her as a competitor for the love of her father, which I craved. To my horror, I began to realize that though I was already in my thirties, I still yearned to be a son and was terrified of being an adult. In the end I couldn't marry Eva and hurt her desperately. It was becoming clear to me that my father's suicide had left a gaping, perhaps irreparable wound.

On one occasion, I became so desperate that I consulted a psychoanalyst. "What would you most like to do with your life?" asked the doctor, not unreasonably.

"Start all over again!" I blurted out completely truthfully.

The doctor shook his head. "Middle age has hit you early," he said gravely. "Apparently you cannot tolerate success. Be careful that you don't destroy what you have built."

"How often would I have to come and see you?" I inquired.

"Five times a week, for at least three years," the doctor said.

"And what is the cost per session?"

"Forty dollars" was the answer.

"That's a lot of time and money," I said, rising from my chair.

"It's a bargain," said the doctor, accompanying me to the door.

Actually, I had found an outlet that relieved my boredom and frustration. The commodities futures market was a highly speculative vehicle that thrilled me in a way that my love affairs no longer did. The stock market did not move fast enough to satisfy my need for action, and straight casino gambling struck me as a bore. The markets in cocoa, soybeans, and silver, on the other hand, were highly volatile and a speculator was required to deposit a margin of only ten percent of the cost of a given futures contract. This made for enormous leverage and lightning action. If one was on the right side of the market, it was quite possible to pyramid a small investment into a modest fortune. If, on the other hand, one had calculated or guessed wrongly, one could expect a margin call before the trading day had run its course.

The fact that more than ninety percent of all speculators in commodities were known to be losers in the end only increased my sense of challenge. After all, my expertise in international relations, I believed, would give me a decisive edge over the ordinary gambler.

I decided to concentrate on cocoa. The cocoa bean was grown primarily in Ghana and Nigeria. I spent long hours studying crop reports, price trends, and the economic policies of Kwame Nkrumah, Ghana's charismatic president. I read the annual reports of leading candy-bar manufacturers in the United States and studied the chocolate-eating habits of adolescents in the Western Hemisphere. Finally, on the basis of several weeks' exhaustive study, I became convinced that a bull market in cocoa was in the offing. Depositing ten thousand dollars in a margin account at a leading brokerage house, I purchased ten cocoa futures contracts.

Almost immediately after my decision, cocoa prices began to rise. Every day, the value of my contracts rose appreciably. I decided to pyramid, and bought ten more contracts with the profits without having to put up any additional deposit. In less than four weeks, I had parlayed my original investment into almost fifty thousand dollars. My confidence in my newfound talent became contagious. Even my broker began to ask for my advice and listened with respect to what I had to say about crop prospects in Ghana.

One day, however, my broker called: "Cocoa's down the limit," he said glumly.

"What the hell is going on?" I asked, not particularly pleased. I was not overly disturbed, however. Cocoa, after all, was entitled to a small correction after its spectacular rise.

"It's been raining unexpectedly in Ghana," the broker said in a knowledgeable tone, "and they think the crop may be larger than expected."

"Who is 'they'?" I asked more irritably. "I don't know," he answered. "I guess 'they' are the weatherpeople."

So that was it. I had omitted the weather factor from my calculations. I decided that this was not an insuperable problem. I remembered that a former student had recently returned to Accra, Ghana, and was working there for a large industrial concern. Fortunately I had kept his address and promptly dispatched a cable in which I inquired whether, for a modest sum, Tom would telegraph me daily weather forecasts from the best available local meteorological sources. "Yes," came the immediate reply. Relaxing, I sat back. Now I would have some firsthand knowledge of the weather in the Ghana cocoa jungles. Confidently, I looked forward to next day's market opening. At seven o'clock a cable arrived from Tom. "Rain stopped," it said, "dry weather forecast for next three days." I chuckled to myself. Obviously, the climb of cocoa prices would now resume in earnest. Maybe there would even be a drought. Impatiently, I waited for the phone to ring. It did, at nine o'clock, one hour before the New York opening.

"Cocoa's down again in London," my broker said sepulchrally. "They are expecting another limit down move in New York."

"But it stopped raining in Ghana," I shouted into the telephone. "How the hell can cocoa be down?"

"They say it's liquidation by disappointed speculators taking profits," he said.

"Who the hell is 'they'?" I screamed. "The chartists," he said and hung up the phone.

I spent the next two weeks in the office of a chart technician. "Fundamentals do not govern the market exclusively," Sam instructed me. "You have to study price movements in order to project future trends." He adjusted his eyeshade and spread out a huge chart with blue, red, and green lines crossing and crisscrossing each other neatly in complex geometric patterns. "Don't worry," Sam said, "my chart indicates a triple bottom for cocoa just about here." He pointed to a spot on his chart not much lower than my purchase price. "It's most unlikely to go lower."

Gratefully, I looked at Sam. My profits had been wiped out during the last two weeks. The fierce leverage was now working in reverse and my capital was threatened. Worse than that, my confidence was badly shaken. It had stopped raining in Ghana ten days ago and still the price of cocoa was going down relentlessly.

I was at my wits' end. Sam, however, managed to dispel my gloom. The triple bottom on his chart surely would not let me down. With new hope I waited for the next trading day. At nine o'clock, unable to wait, I called up my broker.

"What does it look like?" I asked, my heart pounding.

"Down the limit again," he said without expression.

"What about the triple bottom?" I shrieked in a falsetto voice.

"Going through it like a knife through butter. You have a ten-thousand-dollar margin call," he added.

"Sell the goddamn cocoa," I screamed into the telephone. I didn't have the money to meet the call. In fact, I was virtually wiped out. My ten thousand dollars had shrunk to a pittance of less than seven hundred.

"I advise that you place a stop order twenty points down," Sam said. "There should be resistance just above that point."

"Okay," I said, my hope rising again. Surely, the resistance point and the triple bottom would not betray me utterly. At ten o'clock, the phone rang. It was Sam.

"You're out," he said, "they went for the stops."

"Who are 'they'?" I shouted into the phone, choked with rage.

"I don't know," Sam replied a bit unsteadily. "They say it's the large cocoa dealers."

Even though I had been totally wiped out, I still called Sam the next morning. Like a man whose amputated leg still hurt him, I was unable to let go completely. At least let it go down some more, I prayed. Then I could tell myself that I had done right to sell.

"How's cocoa?" I asked Sam, trying to sound indifferent.

"Up the limit," Sam said quietly. The pain that shot through me was so excruciating that I banged down the telephone. Not only had my money gone into the pocket of some anonymous cocoa trader, but my ego was in tatters. I suddenly realized that I knew absolutely nothing, that if I had done the opposite of what my calculations told me, I would now be rich. And, worse than that, I knew that I was unable to let go, that I was hooked like an addict on his daily fix of heroin.

Whenever I went broke trading cocoa or some other commodity, I purged myself by writing yet another book. At times, I would write all night long in order to meet a publisher's deadline. Then, when the book was finished, I became depressed and bored again and soon the unhappy cycle would begin anew. Then I would immerse myself in the latest forecasts about the bacon-eating habits of Americans or the supplies of silver bullion in the mint in Washington. Most of the time, I experienced defeat. Only once, for a brief moment, I tasted an elusive victory. For many months, there had been a widespread rush to buy silver as a hedge against inflation. The speculative fever had become so pervasive that brokers virtually pushed one into silver futures.

Even the elevator operator in my building had decided to invest in silver coins. I sensed that this could not go on forever and went short. It so happened that I was lucky and had hit the top. The market broke sharply for several weeks and I amassed a fair amount of money. That short-lived triumph gave me greater pleasure than did the royalty checks earned by my books. My ego swelled with pride. Shortly afterward, however, I lost most of the silver profits in soybeans. The only time I really beat the system—even if only temporarily—was when I ignored everyone around me and walked straight into the tunnel of my fear. I also knew that my gambling had little, if anything, to do with a desire to get rich. Money was simply a way of keeping score, a way of knowing in a very concrete way whether I was doing well or badly. The action was the thing I craved. Without it, I felt anxious and empty, as if a vital link to life itself had been cut off. Dimly, I perceived the awful truth: What was keeping me alive was also killing me.

Strangely enough, my work did not suffer in those years. I had become a well-known scholar and my books were used as texts on many college campuses. My classes at the college were always filled, and I genuinely liked my students and my colleagues. I had also developed a repertory of public lectures. My reputation was growing and demand for me was steadily increasing.

The book for which I had received the Bancroft Prize had grown out of my life experience. During the first twenty years of my life in Europe and in China, I had been witness to historical tragedy. And during the second twenty years in the United States, I had come to believe that America was still relatively innocent of tragedy.

Americans—even scholars—generally tended to deny this innocence. They would point to the American Civil War of a century ago, to the Great Depression of the 1930s, and to the two world wars. Perhaps my own experiences had altered my perspective, but it seemed to me that what Americans had experienced on a world level *did* bestow on that country a unique kind of innocence. When Americans spoke of World War I, I recalled that the combined Anglo-French losses in a single day at the Somme River were greater than America's losses in *the entire war*, to say nothing of the fact that the war had been waged four thousand miles away from the United States. In World War II, Russia and Germany *each* lost more men at Stalingrad than America lost in all her wars put together. In China I had seen abject, grinding poverty and squalor, and when Americans spoke of their Great Depression, I recalled that in the Depression unemployment had been the crucial problem. But in China, more people were *dying of starvation* at the time than there were Americans being *born* in the United States.

And then there was the Holocaust: the murder of six million European Jews, including one million children. Tragedy was too weak a word to describe this event. There were no words for it. Only memory. For each survivor, his own special hell. For me, my grandparents, falling into their grave—a mass grave.

Innocence. I had been fortunate enough to escape the Holocaust. I owed my life to a man I hated and despised, and I had lost my innocence before I even knew the meaning of the word. And now I was writing about the foreign affairs of a nation where it seemed to me innocence was a terminal disease.

The more I studied the United States and the other super-powers—Russia and China—the more I realized that bridges had to be built between them. Each would have to understand the other's history and culture. If we allowed ourselves to be blinded by simpleminded myths and misconceptions, we were doomed.

The more I brooded on the problem, the worse it seemed. I began to believe that even *understanding* was not enough.

Nations also had to learn to *feel* each other with their souls.
The other alternative—which I, unlike most Americans, had
seen firsthand—was horrendous tragedy, whether it took
the form of nuclear war or the terror of a totalitarian regime.
Intelligence and knowledge alone, I believed, could not
prevent catastrophe. Here I had come to differ with some of
my colleagues very seriously. The old chessboard power
politics had failed. History had moved too quickly. What
was needed now was the kind of empathy that flowed from
the final knowledge that ultimate tragedy was not only
possible but imminent. And from the subsequent realization
in our hearts that all men—in their brief and precarious
journey through life—were either truly brothers or truly
dead.

And yet, it seemed to me that as inevitable as historical
tragedy appeared, there was a paradox inherent in that
tragedy. For if man's history appeared as a gigantic river of
blood, it was also true that on the banks of that bloody river,
people made love, built houses, wrote songs, and sometimes
children laughed and played. Men had built *both* cathedrals
and concentration camps.

And out of this paradoxical, embattled vision, I began to
develop a fascination for the United Nations. Perhaps in
that glass house, people might finally discover that no nation
had a monopoly on virtue, justice, or morality. I remembered
what I had been taught in high school in Austria, Czechoslovakia, and China.

In Vienna I had learned that Austria was the most important nation in the world since, in 1684, an Austrian army
had stopped the Turks at the gates of Vienna and thus saved
Western civilization. But in Prague, the following year, a
Czech teacher had told us that it was a Polish king who had
led the decisive charge against the Turks and that it had
been the Slavic peoples who had been the beacon light of
history. And in Shanghai, a Chinese teacher had informed us
that the Middle Kingdom had been the world's fountainhead

for several millennia and that Europeans and Americans were little better than barbarians. Each country I had lived in had shown a curious tendency to regard itself as the center of the universe.

Gradually, I became more involved in United Nations studies. I became more and more convinced of my idea that nations not only had to "understand," but also "feel" each other, and that therein lay mankind's hope. And that was the United Nations' promise.

I even wrote a book on that theme and the United Nations. And to my surprise, the book won considerable critical acclaim.

Despite my success in academic life, however, or perhaps because of it, I was often desperate. The very real recognition I enjoyed made me feel guilty and uncomfortable. It seemed that every upward step I took elicited a countervailing urge to self-destruct. Only when I fell into the pit did I feel cleansed and purged of guilt. It was almost as if someone with enormous power over me had decreed that my life would be an endless cycle between success and self-destruction.

After I had completed my book on the United Nations, my heart was touched again. I had met Caroline in one of my audiences and, attracted by her smile and expressive gray-blue eyes, asked her for a date. She took me to her little walk-up flat and played Bach preludes for me. I sensed a loneliness in this gentle girl from the South, almost a wordless recognition. We made love that very night and I felt a happiness and freshness that I had thought were gone forever. In the morning, she prepared breakfast on a little terrace full of flower pots.

Caroline had been born in a little town in northern Arkansas. Her father, she told me, had been a conductor and her mother had taught school for thirty years. She had a younger sister, Linda, whose husband had abandoned her and left her penniless with three young children. Caroline had received a scholarship at a conservatory and was aspiring to a career as a concert pianist. Linda, who had been a gifted violinist, was unable to pursue her music because she had to provide for her three children. After Caroline had gone to New York to study, the two sisters had not seen each other for almost seven years.

Caroline persuaded Linda to visit her in New York for a few days. I was invited to join the sisters for an evening at Caroline's apartment. As I walked in, I heard the strains of Beethoven's Spring Sonata for piano and violin. An emaciated-looking woman stood next to Caroline. The sisters played with depth and feeling, but Linda got stuck in a few places. "Let it sing, let it sing," Caroline encouraged her repeatedly.

When they had finished, Linda broke into tears. "She hasn't touched her fiddle in almost seven years," Caroline explained. "But all this is going to change," she added. "I intend to find a job for her in a local orchestra." I was touched and didn't quite know what to do.

"A lot of talent in this family," I said inanely. Linda looked at me. "Which orchestra did your father conduct?" I asked. The surprise on Linda's face gave way to puzzlement. Suddenly, Caroline broke into laughter.

"Our father didn't conduct an orchestra—" she began.

"But didn't you tell me?" I interrupted.

"He was a conductor on the train to Memphis," Caroline explained. The sisters laughed and I laughed with them.

"How about some Mozart?" I asked and reached for Caroline's hand.

Gradually I fell in love with Caroline. I fought it all the way but her gentleness made it hard for me to leave her. When the inevitable moment came and she confronted me with the familiar ultimatum, I could not face yet another separation. Her presence in my life had become a sanctuary.

We made three attempts to get a marriage license and three times I managed to get sick. Several times, I ostentatiously dated other women. Somehow, Caroline endured it all. Finally, on Christmas Eve of 1966, in the middle of a snowstorm, we were married. Professor Morgenthau had consented to be best man. As I kissed my bride, I was no longer fearful. I sensed that this gentle, loving woman with her gift of music might be able to heal the sickness of my soul.

Caroline revealed herself to be a woman with a loving and intelligent heart. She suggested that I remove the nameplate with the title "Dr." from the door of our apartment. "You are a talented and brilliant man," she said, "and you don't have to announce it with a title. Have confidence in yourself."

In the evenings, when I would work, she would usually practice for a concert or recital. I would sometimes interrupt my work and listen. There were fleeting moments when I felt less driven, and experienced a sense of tranquillity and peace.

Over the months, Hans Morgenthau became a frequent visitor. I admired the aging scholar not only for his commitment to his work but also for his courageous opposition to the Vietnam war. He had warned against the dangers of the war earlier than many others and had become the subject of fierce official attacks. It had taken me several years to find the courage to address him by his first name. Gradually, however, I lost my initial shyness and soon the dinner table was not quite complete without his presence.

"Have you heard the story about the sexton in the temple?" Hans asked over dessert, turning to me.

"No," I lied. I had heard it twice before.

"On Yom Kippur," Hans began, "the rabbi falls to the ground, beats his chest and shouts, 'I am nothing.' The cantor, too, falls to the ground, beats his chest and shouts, 'I am nothing.' Suddenly, the little sexton drops to the floor shouting, 'I am nothing.' The rabbi looks at the sexton in consternation. 'Look who says he is nothing,' he whispers to the cantor."

On another occasion, when I praised a not particularly brilliant colleague for his modesty, Morgenthau looked at me skeptically. "He has much to be modest about," he quipped laconically.

Several weeks after my marriage, I received a letter from the State Department. A recruitment officer informed me that a high post in the United Nations Secretariat had opened up and urged me to apply. Somewhat overwhelmed, I hesitated, but Caroline reminded me that the United Nations was something I believed in, and encouraged me to go ahead. I asked for an appointment with U Thant, the secretary-general.

"You would supervise about thirty men and women," said U Thant, "and you would be responsible for the preparation of position papers and political analyses for me on a weekly basis." His kind face broke into a smile. "I have read your latest book on the United Nations," he added, "and I would like it very much if you could work for us."

I felt my ego surge with pride. At last I would be able to enter the world of power and be an adviser to the secretary-general on United Nations policy. I also decided to set up a new institute at the university that would be dedicated to United Nations issues and for which I would raise funds. I thought of Rusty's mother and what she had predicted twenty years ago. I determined to give my new assignments everything I had. Before I wrote my letter of acceptance, I closed my brokerage accounts without a moment of regret. I now had better things to do.

I was assigned a spacious office in the glass house overlooking the East River. A highly qualified Indian secretary was assigned to me. My immediate superior was a Soviet undersecretary who warned me that any paper that was prepared by my division would have to be shown to him before it was transmitted to the secretary-general. "Soviet-American balance," he explained, showing his steel-capped teeth in a large smile.

The officers assigned to me impressed me favorably. Each had a separate office and access to a secretary. The thirty men and women came from many different countries and most of them had either earned higher academic degrees or had had experience in diplomatic posts throughout the world. I found that they responded well to my enthusiasm and they soon began to submit excellent political analyses on a variety of subjects. I would spend long hours in discussion with the members of my staff. Then I would take each paper to the Soviet undersecretary and we would bargain, often fiercely, over every page until, finally, the product of these extensive labors was sent up to the secretary-general. U Thant had his suite three floors above my office, but he might as well have been in a different country. I saw him only rarely after that initial interview, usually at a diplomatic reception where he stood patiently in line shaking a thousand hands with a benign though somewhat frozen smile.

Once, after a particularly sharp debate with the Soviet undersecretary over a paper that I considered to be of great importance, I decided to see U Thant. I wanted to clarify my position orally. A secretary ushered me in almost immediately.

"Well, professor, how is school?" asked U Thant, holding out his hand.

"School is fine, Mr. Secretary-General," I replied, somewhat taken aback, "but may I speak to you about a paper?"

"Oh, yes, of course," U Thant replied, absentmindedly. "How are you getting along?"

"Fine," I answered. "Have you found my papers helpful?"

"I have been terribly busy lately," U Thant said apologetically. "I really haven't had time to get to them. But your work is very useful," he added quickly, after looking at my face.

"Have you seen the recent one we did on the Middle East?" I asked, my heart sinking.

"No, not yet. But do keep up the good work," he repeated, rising from his chair. He held out his hand to me. I looked into his kind and gentle face, and was unable to feel any anger. I took his hand.

"Thank you, Mr. Secretary-General," I said and walked toward the door.

"Professor," I heard U Thant say. I turned around. "In this house," U Thant said quietly, "you must be a philosopher."

I walked down the back stairs to my office. I did not wish to take the elevator since I was not certain whether I could hold back the tears of frustration that were welling up inside me. For two years, I had supervised and written countless papers for an audience of one, and now I had discovered that there was no audience at all. The papers had been sent into a void and were gathering dust in some remote filing cabinet. I thought of my staff of dedicated officers. Their talent was completely wasted, their hard work useless, their salaries paid for nothing. As for myself, my impact had been zero.

The shock to my ego was so overwhelming that I sat down in the middle of the staircase. It occurred to me that this was how the land surveyor in Franz Kafka's *Castle* must have felt. The hero of the Kafka novel died in the process of trying to reach the owner of the castle, by whom he was supposed to be employed. The bureaucratic obstacles that were placed in his path finally were too much for him. Kafka could learn many lessons here, I thought bitterly as I got up from the stairs.

When I re-entered my office, one of my subordinates was waiting. He was a Turk of fierce loyalty and dedication who approached his work with the utmost seriousness.

We had already had half a dozen conferences about some changes on a paper that he had written.

"Last night I thought about what you said, and I have another compromise proposal," Ahmed said.

"Let me see it, Ahmed," I said, my feelings again under control. We talked for half an hour and Ahmed left my office, with a smile of satisfaction. His earnest face had become flushed during the discussion and I had noticed beads of perspiration on his forehead.

"Thank you, Ahmed," I said to him at the door. "Thank you for your excellent work. The secretary-general will appreciate it."

Then I went to the men's room, locked myself in, and cried.

The United Nations Secretariat. I remembered the fierce joy I had felt on my first day of work there. At last, I would be part of a larger integrating cause: the building of a better world order. And now I saw the truth: men and women of often high ideals, confined in a world of glass and steel, doomed to strive in deepening frustration, becoming more and more disconsolate, and finally succumbing to the pension system and a relentless mediocrity. There were exceptions to this rule, of course. And the United Nations was just a mirror of the world's ills. It made little sense to spend one's energies raging at the mirror. The ideals of the UN charter were still valid and certainly worth fighting for. What I understood that day on the back stairs of the Secretariat building, however, was that I wouldn't live to see them actualized.

In 1970, I was invited by Grinnell College to receive an honorary degree and to give the commencement address. I wondered whether the new president knew about the circumstances of my disappearance from the campus twenty years earlier. A great deal had changed at Grinnell since then, and Dr. Stevens had been dead ten years. Two days before commencement day, however, I received a call.

"We have a revolution here on campus," Grinnell's new president said apologetically. "It's about Cambodia; there will be no commencement this year."

"Really?" I asked, not quite knowing what to say.

"We will mail you your degree," the president added. "I am truly sorry."

He sounded quite sincere and either did not know about my past or had written off the 1950 episode as belonging to another era. Two weeks later my honorary doctorate arrived by registered mail, exactly like the undergraduate diploma twenty years before.

Life had settled down once more to a routine. I taught my classes, supervised papers that no one read, and tried to raise money for my anemic institute. Lately, I had begun to work on a new book in my air-conditioned United Nations office. No one seemed to mind. Occasionally, I saw U Thant at a reception.

"We should build a world university," he told me once. I looked at him with renewed interest.

"I would love to help," I said sincerely.

"We would have to raise a lot of money," U Thant said, "and I am not sure if the world is ready for it." The secretary-general, I thought, looked drawn and ill. There was a rumor that he was suffering from cancer.

I had begun to gamble again in cocoa futures. My disappointment with the United Nations and the constant struggle to maintain the institute had thrown me into a depression. I was in my middle forties now and my old problem stared me in the face again, except that I was ten years older. There was nowhere else to go. Caroline suggested, sensibly enough, that I should enjoy the success that I had attained. It was, after all, not inconsiderable. I knew that she was right, but it didn't help me. Somehow, I was unable to reconcile myself to a middle-of-the-road existence. Unless I was at the very top, I thought of myself as absolutely worthless. Inexorably, my depression deepened and I began to flirt again with self-destruction. More than once, I thought of suicide.

Once, on a speaking tour of Florida, I visited an acquaintance in Miami. "I am expecting an overseas call from a business associate in London," said Colonel Flynn. "She has a question about the United Nations; could you talk to her?"

"Why not?" I responded. Shortly afterward, the call came through.

"Her name is Laura Larrabee," Flynn said. "She is an international financier." I picked up the phone.

"I hear you work for the United Nations," said a voice that sounded warm and friendly. "Would you make an inquiry for me at the Mexican mission?"

"Sure," I replied. I liked the way the woman laughed on the telephone. She made one want to laugh with her. Two weeks later, the phone rang in my United Nations office. It was Laura Larrabee. I gave her the information she had asked for.

"I would very much like to meet you," Laura Larrabee said after a brief pause. "I believe in the United Nations and in world peace."

"Of course," I replied. She sounded charming.

"I am arriving at Kennedy Airport the day after tomorrow," said Laura Larrabee. "Could you meet me there?"

I hesitated. Going out to Kennedy would kill an entire afternoon.

"I am frightened by all that confusion at the airport," Laura Larrabee said and laughed. The laughter rippled out like a cascade of silver across the transatlantic wire.

"Fine," I said, "I'll be there."

"I am blond and a little plump," Laura Larrabee laughed and hung up the phone.

The London flight was almost an hour late. I was mildly annoyed. The traffic to the airport had been heavy and I didn't quite know why I was meeting this strange woman coming in from London. But I was curious, and besides, she had a charming laugh. Maybe she would cheer me up. I peered through the glass partition into the area where passengers were checking their luggage through customs. I saw no one that fitted Laura Larrabee's description. Irritated, I placed myself directly in front of the sliding doors through which passengers were beginning to push their luggage carts. Thirty minutes passed, and I was getting angry. Suddenly, the doors slid open and I stared at a blond woman in utter disbelief. She had the face of Lisl, whom I hadn't seen in more than thirty years. The woman walked toward me, her blue eyes smiling.

"I am Laura Larrabee," she said and laughed. Then she held out her hand.

PART II

Chapter Seven

"I have to fly to Vienna soon on business," Laura said. "Do you know anyone there? I don't even speak the language."

We were having lunch in the delegates' dining room at the United Nations. Laura was wearing a pink blouse and a matching skirt. A small golden cross hung suspended between her breasts. She had just eaten a wiener schnitzel and was about to start on a large chocolate ice cream sundae. She ate with gusto and was obviously enjoying herself. I looked at her across the table. Despite her large frame, she was an attractive woman. The resemblance to Lisl was astounding. Laura Larrabee looked up from her ice cream and smiled. She had noticed my appraising glance. "Vienna will be great for my diet," she laughed.

Laura had expressed a desire to see the United Nations on the night of her arrival from London. She had never had the time to see it, she explained. Would I give her a guided tour? As I led her through the Security Council chamber, Laura told me about herself. She had worked for an RCA executive, she said, but had gotten bored after a ten-year stint and had decided to become a financier. She served as middleman, or broker, she explained, between banks and governments that were negotiating large international loans. At present, she was working on behalf of the Austrian and Greek governments, which were interested in borrowing large sums of money.

"I am constantly on the move," Laura said with a sigh. "It's an exciting, but exhausting, business. Sometimes I wish I could take some time off. I would like to study the United Nations; you have aroused my interest."

"Would you like to attend one of my institute seminars tomorrow evening at the university?" I asked, rather flattered.

A distinguished colleague from the United Nations was scheduled to speak at dinner and I was eager to make an impression on this important lady financier. Laura consulted a large black diary and frowned slightly.

"I would love to come, but I am not sure whether I can make it."

"Why don't you call me tomorrow and let me know," I said. "I will reserve a seat for you at the dinner." Suddenly I was eager for her to come.

"Fine," said Laura. "Thank you for the tour; you are a terrific teacher. I learned a lot today."

Laura Larrabee did not call the following day and I assumed, not without disappointment, that I probably would not see her again. As I walked the few blocks from the United Nations to the university, I found myself wishing that she had called. To my pleasant surprise, on entering the dining room, I saw her blond hair at the far end of the bar. She was holding a glass of orange juice and talking to a colleague.

"Hi," she waved to me. "I have just been telling your friend that neither one of us likes alcohol."

"Come and sit at the head table," I said, genuinely delighted.

"Thank you," said Laura, "I look forward to being your student tonight."

I placed Laura next to me at the dinner table. Eager to demonstrate my gifts as a lecturer to my guest, I was annoyed that I was not the main speaker. As it turned out, however, the guest lecturer was stimulating and Laura joined freely in the discussion after dinner. She did so intelligently and with a sense of humor.

"It seems to me that the UN is a pretty poor credit risk," she said to me with a laugh after the meeting. "But you certainly are running a marvelous institute. Thank you for inviting me."

On the way to her hotel, I told Laura about my problems with the institute. "I think I can help you," she said without hesitation. "I know some business people in Europe whom I will ask to make contributions. And if my deal in Vienna goes through," she added after a short pause, "I will set aside a part of my own commissions. I am a businesswoman, but I have a deep commitment to world peace." Her generosity touched me. It seemed genuine and quite spontaneous.

"I have an uncle in Vienna," I said. "He is my one surviving relative from the Nazi Holocaust; I will write him and ask that he show you Vienna."

"You will have to call him," Laura said and laughed. "I am supposed to be in Vienna the day after tomorrow. But why don't you come up and write down his address for me?"

Laura occupied a luxurious suite on the top floor of the hotel. She took off her mink coat and threw it on one of the two double beds. Then she took out her black diary and handed it to me.

"There is room on the last page," she said, handing me a silver pencil.

I sat down at the little hotel desk and jotted down my uncle's name and address. Then I rose and handed the diary and pencil back to her. She took both, but did not let go of my hands. Instead, without an instant's hesitation, she pulled me toward her and kissed me. The diary and silver pencil fell to the floor. I felt her breasts against my body. They were large and firm and I felt a flash of excitement.

"I am married, Laura," I managed to stammer, catching my breath.

"I know," Laura murmured. "You told me that you are happily married. I won't make any demands on you; I am hardly ever in the United States; but this is the first time since I left my husband that I am attracted to a man. I am a proud woman and it is not easy for me to say this, but I want you to make love to me tonight."

Laura unbuttoned her pink blouse and revealed two large breasts that were very white. Then she quickly stepped out of her skirt. I stared at the little golden cross. Laura turned off the light on the little night table, which was adorned with a Gideon Bible.

"Why don't you come to bed," she said, "and don't worry. The first time is always awkward, but we will survive it."

Afterward, Laura kissed me on the cheek.

"Not so bad for two old people in their forties," she said. "I wonder whether your students do as well." I laughed and looked at her. Her blue eyes were mocking me. "I think I will fall in love with you," she suddenly said, her eyes turning serious. "It's never been this good for me."

It was past midnight and I was concerned about Caroline. I did not want to call her from Laura's suite. Suddenly, I felt flooded with guilt.

"Laura," I said, "I have to go home."

"I know," said Laura without a trace of anger. "I will call you from Vienna in a few days. By the way," she added, "I might ask you for a letter of recommendation."

"What do you mean?" I asked.

"A character reference, silly." She laughed and kissed me. "It will help me in your hometown."

"I'll be happy to, Laura," I said. I felt stiff and formal

next to this uninhibited creature. "I'll call my uncle right away; it's already morning in Europe."

"Don't come to the airport tomorrow," said Laura. "I hate goodbyes. But I want you to be there when I get back —whenever that will be."

"Okay, Laurie," I said. Suddenly, I felt touched. I had sensed a vulnerability in this large, self-confident woman. "Have a good trip," I said. The phrase struck me as hollow and a little stupid.

"I'll miss you," said Laura Larrabee. "Now go."

I walked several blocks before I hailed a cab.

"I was getting worried," said Caroline. She had been waiting up for me. "So how was the lady financier?"

"Fine," I replied.

"I heard she is fat and rich. Is that true?" Caroline asked.

"That's right," I said and went to the telephone. "Give me Vienna," I said to the operator.

"Vienna, what?" asked the operator.

"Vienna, Austria," I said.

I hadn't seen my uncle Eddie for more than thirty years. He had emigrated to Australia after the Nazis occupied Vienna and then settled in New Zealand. He had prospered there after the war but was finally so overwhelmed by homesickness for his favorite *kaffeehaus* that, at the age of seventy, he decided to return. A story made the rounds that when he appeared there, the old headwaiter took one look and immediately, without a word, brought Eddie his favorite breakfast: two freshly baked buttered rolls, a soft-boiled egg, and coffee with whipped cream. After an absence of almost three decades, Eddie found this tactful matter-of-fact behavior more touching than the most effusive welcome.

I had not returned to Vienna since the war. There had been no reason for me to do so, nor did I wish to stir up memories. I was acutely aware, however, as I waited on the telephone, that I should long ago have made the effort to contact my dead father's brother. In my heart, I knew that I had not done so for fear of what I might find out about my father.

"Hello," said a voice at the other end.

"Uncle Eddie," I said quickly, "this is your nephew Hans." A strange feeling went through me as I used my childhood name.

"Hans, my God," said the voice on the other side of the Atlantic, "how I would love to see you. Are you coming to Vienna?"

I suddenly realized that Uncle Eddie obviously thought that I was calling to tell him I was passing through Vienna. Why else would I make an overseas call! I felt ashamed.

"Yes," I said without thinking, "I will visit you this summer."

Then I quickly told him about Laura Larrabee. Eddie promised to be helpful.

"Be sure to come," he insisted. "I want to see you once more in this life."

"Yes, Uncle Eddie, of course I will," I heard myself say.

After I hung up, I began to cry. A hand softly touched my shoulder. It was Caroline. There was concern on her gentle face.

"I don't know what the hell I am getting into," I said, trying to stop my tears. "How would you like to visit Vienna this summer?"

Five days later I had an overseas call at the United Nations.

"Happy New Year," said Laura. Her voice was clear and warm. "Your uncle is a lovely man; he has been showing me Vienna; I have a surprise for you!" She laughed and put Eddie on the line.

"You have sent a charming emissary," said Uncle Eddie. "When will I see you?"

"This summer," I said quickly. I suddenly found myself looking forward to seeing the old man.

"We are at the bank," said Laura, who had gotten on an extension. "Things are going very well. Can you send me that letter?"

"Sure, Laurie," I answered. "What shall I say?"

"Well, say that I have an impeccable reputation and that I have closed numerous financial transactions to the satisfaction of both borrower and lender."

"Fine, Laurie," I said. I had copied down the phrase.

"She is both competent and charming," Eddie said to me in German.

"Your uncle is teaching me your native language," said Laura. "It should come in handy when I see you. I miss you, you know," she suddenly said with emotion. "I wish I had a picture of you."

"I will send you my latest book," I answered quickly.

"Terrific," cried Laura, "send me a few extra copies for the bankers here; I will get you some publicity."

"And one for me," said Eddie.

"See you in New York in about six weeks," said Laura. "I am glad I got you together with your uncle."

During the next few weeks, Laura called me periodically at the United Nations. I found myself looking forward to these calls from Vienna, London, or Geneva. On one occasion, she told me that she loved my book. It deserved the widest readership, she said, and she would do her best to get it translated into as many languages as possible. I felt a sudden rush of gratitude. My book had not exactly been a commercial success and was now destined to become a paperback for the college market. Laura had guessed my thoughts. Academic recognition did not satisfy me any longer. What I craved was a quantum leap into literary fame. One bleak afternoon in February, the phone rang. It was Laura, calling from Geneva.

"I am coming through New York tomorrow," she said. "Can you meet me at Kennedy?"

"How long can you stay?" I asked.

"I am changing planes for Mexico," Laura said, "about eight hours."

"I'll be there," I said.

The next day Laura and I were sitting in the lounge waiting for her plane.

"I have a surprise for you," Laura said. "I have spoken to Bobby Sarnoff and suggested to him that RCA distribute your book as a Christmas gift to all its employees and its best customers."

"How is that possible?" I asked, delighted.

"It's logical," said Laura. "Your book is published by Random House and Random House is owned by RCA. RCA is committed to the improvement of communications throughout the world and your book talks about the new openings to Russia and China." I looked at Laura. Her logic seemed impeccable. Henry Kissinger had just returned from China.

"How many copies would that mean?" I asked.

"Guess," said Laura. I hesitated.

"Ten thousand?" I looked at her questioningly. Laura exploded into her silver laugh.

"Guess again," she repeated.

"I have no idea," I said, my heart racing.

"About four hundred thousand," said Laura. "And now kiss me, we haven't got much time."

Full of gratitude for Laura, I was watching the evening news. The president and Henry Kissinger were briefing reporters after their return from China. Soon my book, too, would have its day. Besides, Laura had told me before she left for Mexico that her Austrian transaction would close soon. A second one, in Greece, she said, was also going well. I had given her another letter. Thanks to Laura, my gloom had lifted. I would finally become a well-known author and would be able to finance my pet project at the university. Besides, she was a sensual, attractive woman. There should be no complications with my marriage, since our occasional trysts would not be difficult to hide. I would have both adventure and security, and might even have a crack at literary glory.

After she left for Mexico, Laura called about once or twice a week. At times, she would call me at home in the middle of the night. "A call for you from Teheran, Iran," the operator would say. Groggy with sleep, I would stagger to my study and pick up the telephone. I did not want Caroline to overhear the conversation.

"I just wanted to hear your voice," Laura would say. "This was the only time I could get through."

"How is it going, Laurie?" I said sleepily.

"Fine," she said, "but lately I have been so busy that I hardly slept at all." It's true, I thought, she sounds tired.

"I wish I could see you a bit more often," Laura said sadly.

"So where is she now?" Caroline asked when I came back to bed.

"Teheran," I said.

"My God, maybe she's a spy," said Caroline.

I hope she doesn't suspect anything, I thought as I tried to go back to sleep.

In April, one of these nocturnal calls came in from Rome.

"I have asked for an audience with the Holy Father. I would like to give him a copy of your book."

"Thank you, Laurie," I said, half asleep. "That's wonderful."

"The book project is going well at RCA," Laura continued.

"Thank you, Laurie," I repeated, not quite knowing what to say. There was a brief pause at the other end.

"I will spend Easter weekend in Rome. Do you think you could join me here?"

I hesitated, suddenly fully awake, my mind racing. I desperately wanted to say yes but did not wish to hurt Caroline. Confronted with the classic married man's dilemma, its banality and my own cowardice repelled me.

"Do you think you can get away?" I heard Laura say. Her voice sounded small and almost plaintive. It occurred to me that I had not heard her laugh for quite some time. Suddenly, I felt touched by this woman who seemed so self-assured and yet so vulnerable.

"Of course I'll come, Laurie," I heard myself say.

"Terrific. Meet me at the Excelsior Hotel."

"I'll be there," I said.

"And bring some more books, I have run out, and some stationery; I may need a few more letters." She laughed her silvery laugh.

"Of course I will," I said.

"Laura Larrabee wants me to come to Rome," I said to Caroline at breakfast. "She is placing a large order of my book with RCA."

Caroline looked at me quizzically. "RCA is in New York," she said. "Why do you have to go to Rome?"

"She is helping me finance the UN institute," I said, "and she needs me there on business."

"What do you know about her business?" Caroline persisted. I felt my anger rising. Caroline's questions were both innocent and logical.

"She wants me to meet a Vatican official," I said, "who is interested in my book." It was a stupid lie which had occurred to me instinctively, without reflection. Caroline looked at me with her gentle eyes. I saw the hurt in them and realized that she knew the truth. A sinking feeling came over me. But I had made a commitment and was no longer able to turn back. Caroline lapsed into a heavy silence. I was grateful that she didn't make a scene. But even if she had begged me on her knees, I suddenly realized with horror, I would still get on that plane to Rome.

Even though my guilt was great, the temptation to go was even greater. A pretty woman who reminded me of my boyhood love and who had promised to make my dreams come true had invited me for a holiday in Rome. For six years, I rationalized, I had been a loving husband to my wife. Surely, I was entitled to a weekend of adventure after years of discipline and work.

"When will you come back?" asked Caroline, reaching for my hand.

"In three days, maybe four," I said, packing a small valise and avoiding my wife's eyes. Then, fighting my guilty conscience, I left the house and jumped into a cab.

Laura was waiting for me at the airport. She had lost weight and looked pretty in a fluffy woolen sweater. She kissed me, her blue eyes sparkling. In the cab, on the way to the hotel, she showed me a letter. It was from the secretary of state of the Vatican. In it the official thanked Laura Larrabee for having transmitted a copy of my book to the Holy Father.

"The Pope gave me an audience," Laura added. "I told him how much I believed in your work and he gave me his blessing."

I looked at Laura. Her face was serious and almost beautiful. The little golden cross was shimmering in the bright Italian sun. I was glad that I had come to Rome.

We were sitting in a small café on the Via Veneto. It was a warm spring afternoon and the avenue was crowded with strollers taking in the sun. Laura took my hand and looked at me.

"I have good news for you," she said. "Bobby Sarnoff has approved the book project; the capital appropriations board of RCA has set aside the funds; they want to make it a gift for Christmas 1972." Gratefully, I looked at Laura. "What do you think of this?" she asked. She had placed a print of Albrecht Dürer's etching *Hands in Prayer* on the little coffee table. "We want to place this in every copy of the book with a Christmas message from the president of RCA. Could you draft one or two paragraphs for him?" she asked, her eyes laughing. "After all, you are the author." Overcome, I nodded in agreement.

"Tomorrow night I fly to Athens," Laura added. "I hope to close a large loan there with the Bank of Greece. If I succeed, I will set aside half a million dollars for your UN institute." I felt the tears well up within me.

"Laurie," I said, "I don't know what to say, it's all too much for me to grasp."

"I love you," said Laura. Suddenly, her face had become serious. "I love you in a way that I have never loved another man. And I want to make you happy."

"I have a small token for you too, Laurie," I said, taking a little box out of my pocket. Before I had left New York, I had gone to a jeweller and bought Laura a string of pearls. I placed the necklace around Laura's neck and kissed her. Laura did not look at the pearls but continued to look at me: "I love you," she repeated. Then, hand in hand, we walked down the Via Veneto.

"I am a little afraid of going to Greece," said Laura. We were lying in bed and she was cuddling up to me. "They have a police state there. I think you'd better give me a letter of protection."

"Of course I will, Laurie. I wish I could go with you. What do you want me to say?"

"Can you say that I work for you?" Laura asked.

I thought for a moment. "I can appoint you as an intern without salary to my peace research unit at the UN," I said. It was a practice I had followed with some of my better graduate students. "And I can put you on the board of my UN institute at the university since you will raise some funds."

"That's great," said Laura. "Then, if I get in trouble with the junta, you won't have to rescue me."

In the morning, Laura took a portable typewriter from

her valise. She sat down naked at the desk and typed two letters. She typed with such speed that her breasts vibrated with the motion. The sight of Laura, naked and adorned with my string of pearls, pounding at a typewriter with utmost concentration, was too much for me. I burst into helpless laughter.

"Where did you learn to type so well?" I asked her, unable to stop.

"I used to be a secretary," Laura replied with mock pride. "The skill still comes in handy, as you can see." She handed me the letters. With tears of laughter still in my eyes, I signed my name to them.

We were to meet a Vatican official for lunch. Monsignor Conti, Laura told me, was most interested in my book and might be helpful with publicity. We had just settled at a table in a fashionable restaurant on the Via Veneto when a dignified man dressed in a flowing robe approached the table.

"Monsignor," said Laura with a smile of recognition, "please join us."

"Dottore," said the monsignor, after Laura had introduced me, "your book is truly excellent. Truly!" he repeated, shaking my hand.

"Thank you, Monsignor," I said, genuinely pleased.

"Even though I am with the church, I have retained a secular interest in reading," Conti said.

"Your English is excellent, Monsignor," I said, quite truthfully.

"Oh, I know your country well, Dottore," Mr. Conti said. "The signora once showed me New York City." He motioned toward Laura and showed a row of even teeth in a friendly smile.

"Signorina," Laura corrected him with a little laugh. "I am no longer married, Monsignor."

If Conti registered Laura's remark, his face did not betray it. I looked at Laura with admiration. I would never have dared to be that frank with a Vatican official. Suddenly, stung by guilt, I thought of Caroline. I had been out of touch with her for more than forty-eight hours. In the six years of our marriage, this had never happened. I hadn't even lied to her completely, I thought guiltily. Now I had really met a Vatican official.

"When is your plane to Athens?" I asked Laura.

The Athens flight was scheduled to leave one hour before my own departure for New York. As it turned out, however, Laura's flight was delayed and it was she who saw me off.

"Thank you, Laurie," I said. "Thank you for everything."

"I'll call you from Athens," Laura said. "I should be in New York sometime before the summer. When I get there, I will put the final touches on our book project, and I think that your problems with the institute are over." I kissed her. "This will bring me luck in Greece," said Laura, pointing to her necklace.

I walked up the ramp, turned around and waved. As I took my seat on the large jumbo jet, I had a strange sensation. Something had been missing when I had kissed Laura goodbye. I remembered as the plane swung out to sea. She had replaced her little golden cross with my pearl necklace.

Chapter Eight

"A call for you from Athens," said the overseas operator. It was a sunny afternoon in May and I was sitting in my UN office editing a paper.

"Hi," I heard Laura say. Her voice sounded a bit impatient. "I have mixed blessings to report," she said. "The governor of the Bank of Greece just had a heart attack; he is seventy-eight years old. We had to postpone the closing and I'll have to come back to Athens."

"You mean you went to Greece for nothing?" I asked.

"That's right!" Laura sounded frustrated. "And the Austrians are also being difficult."

"So maybe I can show you Vienna if you have to go back there," I said, trying to cheer her up.

"But there is some good news, too," Laura said, her voice brightening. "I am flying to New York tomorrow and you and I will see the president of RCA. Did you compose the Christmas message for the book?" she asked.

"It's been waiting for you on my desk for the last six weeks," I answered happily.

Not unexpectedly, relations between myself and Caroline had become strained since my return from Europe. Caroline had been deeply hurt by my escapade in Rome. It was the first time that dissonance was jarring our marriage. I loved my wife but was simply unwilling to give up my mistress. I hoped that by maneuvering adroitly I would be able to hold on to both. Since Laura never spent more than a day or two in New York City, the traffic problem, in my judgment, would not be insurmountable. "How long can you stay?" I asked Laura on the telephone. "About a week this time," Laura replied.

I had bought myself a new suit at one of New York's leading stores. I wanted to look my best for a luncheon that Laura had arranged with the president of RCA. We were to discuss the Christmas message for the book and to sign an agreement for my royalties. I was in a fever of anticipation. At one dollar per copy, Laura had said, my royalties would come to four hundred thousand dollars. At eleven o'clock, the phone rang.

"Bobby had to cancel," Laura said. "There was an unexpected crisis. Why don't you and I have lunch together at the UN?"

"Fine," I said, trying to hide my disappointment.

"There are a couple more letters that I need," Laura said. "Your secretary might as well type them up while I am there."

Laura greeted me with a discreet kiss.

"Bobby has agreed to see us tomorrow," she said during lunch.

"Laurie," I said hesitantly, "four hundred thousand copies is a gigantic order. I should tell my editor at Random House about it so that they can get them ready."

"Good idea," Laura replied. "The books should be shipped by November. By the way," she continued, "why don't you just write me a couple of 'To Whom It May Concern' letters; then I don't have to bother you every time I need a letter."

"Sure," I replied, "let's go up to the office."

"They can be identical to the ones I typed for you in Rome," Laura said with her silvery laugh. "They will be of help to me in Athens and Vienna."

In the afternoon I saw my editor at Random House. Barry rubbed his forehead thoughtfully. "We can do it by November," he said after a pause. "It's a fantastic opportunity."

"Once in a lifetime," I agreed.

"We have the plates; all we have to do is print 'em," Barry said. "So just give us the go-ahead."

"In a day or two, I hope," I said.

It was eleven o'clock the following morning and I was wearing my new suit again. "Bobby's done it again," said Laura, "but he says tomorrow without fail." I swallowed the anger that I felt rising in me. After all, I supposed, it wasn't Laura's fault that the chief executive of RCA had more important things to do than meet with a middle-aged author.

"But now that we have a couple of hours to spare, you can do me a small favor," Laura said with a laugh.

"What can I do for you, Laura?" I asked, trying to sound natural.

"Can you open a special bank account, giving me power of attorney? It's just a matter of convenience; you could pay some petty bills for me while I am gone; I will make the deposits."

"I suppose so," I replied, taken aback a little. "I will ask my friendly banker."

We went to my bank and I asked to see the manager.

"There is no problem," said the bank official. "The lady will make the deposits, but you, professor, will receive the monthly statements."

"That's fine with me," I said to Laura. "I'll save the monthly statements for you."

"While we are here," said Laura, "why don't you open a safe deposit box? I'd like to put some of my valuables in it." Surprised, I looked at Laura. "I fly a great deal," Laura explained, "and I carry too many documents around with me."

We went to the rear of the bank and a clerk filled out the necessary forms. Laura placed some papers in the box and I received the key.

"If one of these days my plane should crash, you are the executor of my will," Laura said to me in a serious tone. "You are the only person in the world whom I really trust." I felt myself blush violently.

"Laurie," I said, "I am not a lawyer, I really don't understand these things."

"All the better," Laura said, erupting into peals of laughter, "all the better because lawyers would only divide up the loot among themselves. And now come home with me."

The following day, I sat in my office, unable to work. Caroline had made a scene the night before and the guilt was strangling me. I was afraid to analyze my feelings honestly. I was not in love with Laura. I was in love with Caroline. Yet I was hurting my wife desperately because Laura had become my key to fame and power. If I could only learn to walk the tightrope, I thought, I would be able to still that hunger that had been eating out my guts. Suddenly, it occurred to me that I was behaving like a whore. Worse than a whore, I thought, because whores had no one to come home to while I had a wife whose love and trust I was using as a crutch for my adventures. What if Caroline left me? I began to wonder. Would I exchange her for a life with Laura?

The telephone interrupted my train of thought.

"I am afraid to tell you this," said Laura, "but Bobby suddenly had to leave town."

"To hell with Bobby," I screamed into the telephone, "and to hell with your damn promises!" I was hardly able to control my rage. "I suppose he will see us tomorrow," I said sarcastically in a calmer tone.

"No," said Laura, "I have to leave the day after tomorrow. We'll have to meet with him when I get back." Laura had begun to sob on the telephone. "May I come over for lunch?" she asked. Her voice sounded pitiful, almost like that of an abandoned little girl.

"Laura," I said, still furious, "please don't make me promises you cannot keep. It hurts too much."

"Why don't you trust me?" Laura sobbed. She had begun to weep uncontrollably. Torn between rage and pity, I didn't quite know what to say.

"Why don't we wait till tomorrow, then?" said Laura. Her voice was small and plaintive as she hung up the phone. Wracked by guilt toward both my wife and mistress, I slumped down in my chair.

"So how was RCA?" asked Caroline when I sat down at dinner. "Did she make you into a great author yet?" I didn't answer. I was too sick with guilt and rage. "I wouldn't count my royalties if I were you," said Caroline.

Next morning, at ten o'clock, the phone rang in my office. Thinking it was Laura, I picked it up myself, not waiting for my secretary. It was my banker.

"I have some interesting news for you," he said, "someone has just deposited a cashier's check for fifty thousand dollars in your account."

"Who?" I stammered, knowing full well what he would say.

"Miss Laura Larrabee," the banker said.

Laura and I were sitting in my favorite Chinese restaurant near the UN. She had called me minutes after I had received the call from my banker.

"I can't talk long," she had said breathlessly. "Please meet me for dinner tonight."

"I had the feeling that you didn't believe me," Laura said reproachfully. "So I went to my private vault."

"Laura," I said, "I don't want your money, but I had my heart set on the book project."

"The money is a loan, you can pay it back after Christmas when you get your royalties," Laura said a little sharply. She opened her purse and took out a rectangular printed form that looked like a check. "This is an IOU for fifty thousand dollars. Sign it, the money is an advance on your royalties."

I hesitated. I didn't really need the money. A stock that I had bought a few months ago had recently tripled in value. On the other hand, I thought, if I accepted the advance, RCA would be more likely to deliver on its commitment. I looked at the IOU. It was made out to Laura Larrabee.

"But, Laurie," I said, "these are your personal funds."

Laura picked up a briefcase which was lying on the seat next to her and opened it. I looked at dozens of stock certificates in various colors. Laura picked up one of them and held it up in front of me. It was a certificate for one hundred thousand shares of stock made out to Laura Larrabee.

"This piece of paper alone is worth close to a million dollars," Laura said. "I built the company together with my husband, but I left him when he began to bore me." Laura's voice suddenly had an edge to it that I had never heard before. "Fifty thousand dollars is peanuts for me," she said, her voice rising. "But what hurt me is that you doubted my word. Now sign the note." She had thrust a pen into my hand. "And, by the way, I haven't forgotten the contribution to the institute," she added. "You will get that, too. You will get half a million dollars as soon as I close my deal."

"Okay, Laurie," I said, "but I would still like to meet Mr. Sarnoff."

"You will, damn it," Laura snapped. "I wish you wouldn't push me so hard; you know that I am leaving tomorrow."

"Well, anyway," I said a little timidly, "here is the Christmas message that I drafted." Laura folded it up without reading it and put it in her purse.

"I am leaving tomorrow," she repeated. "Isn't there anything else we can talk about?"

"Come, I'll take you home," I said, and signed the note.

"Well, what do you say now?" I asked Caroline later as I showed her the deposit slip for fifty thousand dollars. My need to prove to her that I was on my way to literary stardom had made me tactless. Besides, Caroline had sulked around the house for weeks and the icy atmosphere had begun to be unbearable. "We can get you a concert grand now," I said, trying to bribe her into a smile. Caroline made no response.

"How about a trip to Europe?" I asked. "I would love to show you Vienna." Caroline's face lit up.

"I have always wanted to see the city of Mozart and of Schubert," she said. Her voice was small and sad.

"Let's go, then," I said, taking her in my arms, "let's have another honeymoon." Caroline nodded and tears began to roll down her face. "We will leave in a week," I said, holding her and kissing her eyes. I knew that I still loved her insofar as I was capable of love at all.

The large Pan Am plane was about to touch down in Vienna. Choked with emotion, I held on to Caroline's hand. Below us lay the ancient city which had honored both Beethoven and Hitler. The spire of St. Stephen's Cathedral came into view.

"That's where I heard Mozart's C Minor Mass for the first time," I whispered to Caroline.

"We'll visit it together," said my wife and squeezed my hand.

We were planning to spend two weeks in Vienna on our way to Russia. The Soviet government had invited me to give some lectures at Moscow University during the summer. I wished to keep my promise to visit Uncle Eddie and also wanted to patch up my relationship with Caroline. I had told Laura about my Russian lecture tour before she left for Europe, but I had not said anything about visiting Vienna.

A portly man with a balding head came toward us at the gate.

"Hans," he said, his eyes moist with tears, "you look exactly like your father. Even without the picture I would have recognized you right away." The large man hugged me to him as if I were his son.

"Uncle Eddie," I said, a bit embarrassed, "this is my wife Caroline."

"Enchanted," said Eddie in a courtly manner that seemed completely natural, and he kissed Caroline's hand.

We drove into town in Uncle Eddie's Volkswagen. Vienna hadn't changed too much, I thought, as we approached the Ringstrasse. Despite his seventy-five years, Eddie was a skillful driver. He stopped the car on a narrow side street and got out.

"We are not home yet," he said, a little out of breath. "I just want to buy some cold cuts for dinner."

I looked at Caroline. I knew that Uncle Eddie had a wife. It seemed a bit peculiar that she hadn't prepared a home-cooked meal.

A small birdlike woman with a heavily lined face opened the door.

"Good evening," she said formally, shaking my hand without a smile.

"I bought a chicken and some potato salad," said Eddie. His wife nodded.

"You can set the table," she said, "and I will make some coffee. Or would you prefer tea?" she asked, turning to me.

"Yes, tea, please," said Caroline, noticing my hesitation. I was not a coffee drinker but Eddie's wife had managed to intimidate me.

"If you two need a chauffeur," said Eddie, "I am available all day." He bit into a chicken leg. "I am retired and nothing would give me greater pleasure."

"Thank you, Uncle Eddie," I said, "that would be wonderful." Suddenly, I felt sorry for the old man. He seemed desperately lonely. I sensed a wall of ice between him and his wife.

"How about tomorrow?" Eddie asked, looking at Caroline. "I could drive you out to Heiligenstadt; we could visit Beethoven."

During the next few days Eddie drove us all over Vienna. He was affectionate and often placed his arm around my shoulder in a warm and spontaneous gesture; to Caroline he was considerate and solicitous. His wife never came along. She had not been well lately, Eddie said on one occasion; then he never mentioned her again. Despite his genuine warmth and an infectious sense of humor, I sensed a profound sadness about Eddie.

"I think you should talk to him," Caroline said to me after one of our drives into the Vienna woods. "I think he wants to be alone with you. And we won't be here much longer."

Eddie and I were sitting in the *kaffeehaus*. It was ten o'clock on a weekday morning and the place was almost empty. The headwaiter had just brought our breakfast on a silver tray and had withdrawn silently with a respectful bow. Eddie was stirring his coffee.

"Your father and I used to come here more than forty years ago," he said suddenly. "You know, I loved your father very much."

"Eddie," I said, mustering up all my courage, "how did it happen? Was it because of the Nazis?"

Eddie kept stirring his coffee. "No," he answered, "it was before the Nazis." I looked up in surprise. "It was over money and a woman.

"It was during the depression in 1931," Eddie began. "Karl

—I mean your father—was heavily in debt. The creditors were beating down his door, and in his despair, he did something stupid: He gave one of his creditors a large check." Eddie cleared his throat and hesitated before going on. "Anyway, the check bounced because there was no money in the account and he was arrested for fraud."

"My God," I said, "couldn't he have borrowed the money from someone?"

"He tried, but no one would lend it to him," Eddie said. "So he went to jail." He stirred his coffee again. I noticed that the cup was almost empty. "And there was something else," Eddie said with a sigh. "Your father had an affair with another woman. Your mother found out about it and became hysterical."

"What do you mean?" I asked. "Did she leave him?"

"Yes," Eddie answered. "An unfaithful husband who was in jail was too much for her. She told him that she would leave him and take you with her." I felt a black rage welling up inside me.

"When he got out of jail, after a few months," Eddie continued, "your mother wouldn't take him back."

"And his lady friend?" I asked. I was too embarrassed to refer to the woman as my father's mistress.

"She had disappeared," Eddie replied.

"And so he was alone?" I asked.

"That's right," Eddie nodded sadly. "And in a moment of despair he did it."

"How?" I asked after a pause.

"He swallowed poison," Eddie said and looked at me. I noticed that his eyes had filled with tears. Shaking, I reached for my uncle's hand. "He loved your mother," Eddie choked out, weeping. I held my uncle's hand for a very long time, not knowing whether I was comforting him or trying to draw strength from him. A surge of hopeless love for this old man swept over me, like a memory of distant pain.

"Would you like to visit him?" Eddie's eyes searched mine. I looked at him questioningly. "The cemetery is not too far from here. I've been there twice already since I've come back."

Wordlessly, we rose from the table and left the small café. Eddie took the highway that led out of the city. "He is not in the municipal cemetery," he said. The explanation sounded more like an apology.

Soon we were in the suburbs and I no longer recognized the streets. Finally, Eddie turned into a narrow country road and stopped at the entrance of a tiny cemetery. We walked through the gate and I saw hundreds of little gray stones with names and dates in no particular order. Eddie had begun to walk faster, his eyes fixed on the ground.

"He is all the way at the end," he said apologetically. We walked to the back fence of the cemetery and there, bunched closely together in the corner, were about a dozen little stones. They were clearly separated from the rest by a low fence, almost like pariahs.

"Why is he here like this?" I asked Eddie. I knew the answer, but for some reason, I had to ask the question anyway.

"This is the plot for suicides. They are not allowed to be buried in sanctified ground."

I looked at the little marker which bore my father's name and the year 1932. My mind was racing, but my heart felt numb. It was as if a part of me had been split off. I forced myself to look once more at the little stone. How strange, I thought, that the corpse that had been buried here forty years ago had made me what I was. He was still able to reach out and affect my life after there was literally nothing left of him. It seemed insane.

"How long do skulls last in the ground?" I asked Eddie. My uncle looked at me, surprised. I looked away, ashamed of my tactless question.

Eddie drove back in silence.

"At least we know where he is buried," he said finally. "More than we can say about six million other Jews who were murdered by the Nazis."

"Or about Mozart," I added in a lame attempt at humor. A wordless glance from Eddie told me again how tactless I had been.

"Your Laura is a good businesswoman and I think she is in love with you," Eddie said suddenly, without transition. "But you should be careful," he added thoughtfully, "you have a beautiful and loving wife." Embarrassed and taken by surprise, I sank back in my seat. "I speak from experience," Eddie said, "I couldn't give up women either and finally Lola had enough." Eddie turned onto the highway leading back into the city. "We are like two strangers now, living in the same house."

"Seems to run in the family," I answered.

"What do you mean?" Eddie asked.

"Women," I replied.

Suddenly Eddie broke into a laugh. Gratefully, he touched my arm. My answer had apparently released the tension.

Soon we were back in the inner city.

"I have to buy some cold cuts," Eddie announced, getting out in front of a small delicatessen. We both burst into laughter.

"I am so glad you came to see me," Eddie said. "It's like being with my brother." Suddenly, a shiver went through me.

"I am glad I came, Uncle Eddie," I managed to say haltingly. "But in two days we are off to Russia."

"Please come through Vienna on your way back to New York," Eddie said. His voice was almost pleading. I looked at the old man picking up his dinner from the delicatessen counter.

"Of course I will come back," I said.

On our way to Russia, we stopped in Prague. A pervasive grayness hovered over the old city. Caroline and I looked down on the Moldau River from one of Prague's majestic bridges. I was overcome by sadness. Charles Jordan, who had helped me to America, had been murdered in Prague five years before. His body had been found floating in the Moldau. He had been helping Jews escape from Czechoslovakia to Israel. Rumor had it that the Soviet secret police had collaborated with Palestinian Arabs in his murder.

After a day's stay we left Prague. I felt too unhappy in the city I had once loved so much.

The next day, we arrived in Moscow. Intourist put us up in a cavernous hotel near Red Square. While I was lecturing, Caroline was inspecting music schools. At night we fell into bed, totally exhausted. One evening, we were unable to find our room and a bellhop had to help us.

"Largest hotel in the world," he said proudly, pocketing a tip.

The night before we left, just before dawn, the phone rang.

"Who could be calling us at this hour?" Caroline said sleepily.

I picked up the receiver and heard a silvery laugh.

"I am calling you from Zurich," said Laura. "It took me a few days to track you down." I felt myself breaking out into a sweat.

"That's nice," I whispered into the receiver.

"I know you can't talk," said Laura, "but I just wanted to tell you that I plan to be in New York in about a week."

"That's nice," I repeated, sweating even more profusely.

"I have good news about the book project and the institute," Laura said happily.

"I am looking forward to the lecture," I replied, glancing over at Caroline, who had sat up in bed.

"Don't forget me," said the silvery voice. I heard a click. Laura had disconnected.

"Who was it?" Caroline asked sleepily.

"The secret police," I answered, in a nocturnal attempt at humor. I noticed that I was drenched in perspiration. Trembling, I crept back into the bed and cuddled up to Caroline. She did not move away. Soon I fell asleep and dreamt about Eddie. There was something strange about him. He was looking at me imploringly and trying to tell me something. Yet, no matter how I tried, I couldn't understand. He seemed to be speaking in a language I had never heard before. I woke up suddenly, badly frightened. The dream had had a nightmare quality. Then with a flash of terror I remembered: In the dream, Eddie had looked at me with the face of my dead father.

Chapter Nine

"Now please don't get angry," Laura said. "There is something I must tell you." We were lying in bed, completely spent. I had met Laura at the airport and she had told the driver to take us to the International Hotel. "I can't wait till we get into the city," she had said. In the room, she had practically torn my clothes off. "It's been too long, much too long," she had moaned. "You have a wife, but I have no one."

It had been almost four months since I had seen Laura. A few days after Caroline and I returned from Russia, Laura had called from Geneva and announced that she would be delayed. "Those damn closings," she had said, "there is always some last-minute hitch." She had asked for several more letters, which I mailed to Zurich and Geneva. With each call, my anxiety increased since Laura had failed to mention the book project or any contributions to the institute. My editor at Random House had telephoned me twice and inquired whether he could go ahead. I told him that there had been a delay. "I hope it won't take too much longer," he had warned me. "It'll take time to print four hundred thousand copies." I had also told colleagues at the university that I expected a large funding for the UN insti-

tute. There, too, I had to give evasive answers. Not wishing
to arouse Laura's anger, I had not mentioned my concern
to her in our transatlantic conversations. But now it was
October and only a crash schedule could meet a Christmas
deadline.

"You've been very tactful not to press me," Laura said
after a long pause. "But you mustn't think that I've forgotten." I looked at her gratefully. "The problem is that
someone has to follow up the project step by step at RCA.
Bobby delegated that job to me, but I simply didn't have
the time. So now it's too late for Christmas 1972." I nodded,
my heart sinking. "For that reason," Laura continued, "we
have decided to postpone it to Christmas 1973." I glanced
at Laura, my spirits rising. "I'd like you to meet a friend of
mine at RCA who will help with the project when I am
out of the country. No, there will be no more luncheon
cancellations." Laura took my hand and laughed her silvery
laugh. "I've asked Bernard Hewitt to meet with us tomorrow. Can you make it?"

"Of course," I answered.

"He is a nice and efficient man," Laura said, "and I have
given him precise instructions what to do."

"Thank you, Laurie," I said, relieved.

Without daring to admit it to myself, I had practically
given up all hope. Laura's announcement that the project
had been postponed thus was not a shock but a reprieve.

"I am glad, Laurie," I said. "What you say makes sense
to me; but you'll have to wait another year till I pay you
back the fifty thousand dollars."

"Don't worry about that," Laura said, "you can donate
it to your institute on my behalf when you get your
royalties."

The next day we were sitting in a restaurant near Rocke-
feller Plaza.

"Bernie will be in charge of doing the legwork on the
project," Laura said.

Bernard Hewitt was a mild-mannered black gentleman with a courteous demeanor. As he sat down at our table, he handed me his card. The RCA symbol was embossed on it in large red letters. Underneath it, I read his name: Bernard Hewitt, Staff Services.

"Bernie was a real friend to me when I worked at RCA," Laura said. "He protected me against the corporate hyenas." She and Hewitt chuckled, apparently enjoying an amusing recollection. "He has promised to see to it that the books are properly wrapped and mailed," she added. "With four hundred thousand copies, that'll be quite a job."

"I am most grateful to you, Mr. Hewitt," I said, handing him an inscribed copy of my book.

"I've seen it," Mr. Hewitt said politely. "Miss Larrabee has shown it to me, but I am glad to have an autographed copy of my own."

"When I am out of touch and you want to know what's going on, just call Bernie," Laura said and laughed. "I am off again tomorrow."

"Where to, for God's sake, Laurie?" I asked in consternation.

"To Singapore," Laura said.

"I know the former UN ambassador there," I said after a moment's thought. "Would you like his address?"

"That would be most helpful," Laura said.

Then I took her home.

"I am exhausted and my health has not been good," Laura said. We were eating chicken with snowpeas in our favorite Chinese restaurant. It was shortly after New Year's and Laura had just arrived from Asia. "I am thinking of settling in Toronto," Laura continued. "Would you visit me there if I did?"

My life had settled down once more to a routine. I taught my classes, was hard at work on a new book, and performed my functions as a bureaucrat at the United Nations. Occasionally, I telephoned Mr. Hewitt at RCA. He was always courteous though somewhat noncommittal. "Things are going well," he would say. "Laura is in touch with me about the project."

The usual financial worries were irritating me in connection with the institute. My home life had improved somewhat. As Laura passed through New York less and less often, Caroline's anger had subsided. I could not deny, however, that I looked forward to Laura's brief visits with a deep and secret thrill. They managed to dispel my boredom like shots of distilled adrenaline.

"I would love to visit you, Laurie," I said with sincerity. The prospect of seeing her a bit more frequently appealed to me. Besides, if she settled in Toronto, I could hide our affair more easily from Caroline.

"I am thinking of taking over a business there," said Laura. "In fact, I am having dinner with John Ashley tomorrow and I would like you two to meet; he is a very nice man."

"Okay, Laurie," I said. My voice must have betrayed reluctance because Laura smiled and placed her hand on mine.

"Don't worry," she said, "it's strictly business. He has a studio in Toronto and you might be able to do some educational TV."

"Fine," I said, relieved, "the three of us can have dinner here tomorrow. But now let me take you home."

"My next trip will be a long one," Laura said later. We were resting in bed in her hotel. I was in an irritable mood. Our lovemaking had been interrupted twice by overseas telephone calls. Despite her passionate sexual nature, Laura had a disconcerting habit of disengaging herself even on the verge of orgasm when she heard the telephone. Her transition to a businesslike "Hello" on those occasions was so perfect and immediate that it aroused both my admiration and my anger. I would sulk then and wait for her to return to bed. But often I had difficulty getting back into the mood. Laura, on the other hand, was always ready to continue exactly at the point where we had stopped. "Sorry," she would say with a small laugh.

"How long will you be gone this time?" I asked Laura, a little irritably.

"I think it might be as long as half a year," said Laura. I sat up and looked at her. She was playing nervously with her pearl necklace. "The Austrian transaction has fallen through," Laura said, "and the Greeks are being difficult. I have decided to concentrate on the Middle East and Africa."

"My God," I said, genuinely disconcerted. The book project had flashed through my mind. It would be almost autumn, then, before I would see Laura again.

"This may well be my final trip," Laura said. "I am thinking of taking over Mr. Ashley's business."

"You mean you will run a studio?" I asked in amazement.

"No," Laura replied. "I'll hire someone to take care of the nuts and bolts for me, but I wouldn't mind living in Toronto. It's a lovely city and it's not too far away from you."

"I am almost finished with a new book," I said, hoping that Laura would get the point.

"Oh, that reminds me," she said, "be sure to bring a copy of your book along tomorrow for John Ashley."

Laura and Mr. Ashley were sitting in a booth in the Chinese restaurant when I arrived. Both were drinking scotch. "Good evening," I said a little stiffly. It was the first time that I had seen Laura drink alcohol.

"I hear that you have done educational TV," said Mr. Ashley.

"That's right," I answered, ordering a wonton soup.

"Would you like to do some programs in Canada?" he asked. John Ashley was a pleasant-looking man with a ruddy face and sandy hair.

"Sure," I said, "I could give some lectures on the United Nations or on China."

"He is a great teacher," said Laura. "Here is his latest book." John Ashley looked at the inscription.

"Thank you," he said sincerely. "I will look after her for you." Surprised, I glanced at Laura.

"We are leaving for London," said Laura, reaching for my hand. "But I will see you for lunch before we leave," she added with a smile.

"I am afraid we have to talk business for a few more hours," said John Ashley.

I looked at my watch. "I guess I have to go," I said. Actually, I had no plans of my own. But I felt a sullen anger. Laura was in New York for two days and would be gone for half a year. Yet, she preferred to spend the evening with a stranger talking business rather than in bed with me. As I left the restaurant, my anger deepened. She'll be traveling with him, I thought in consternation. Suddenly, I felt a sharp pang of jealousy. The fact that my reason told me that this jealousy was preposterous and probably unjustified did not alleviate the pain.

The following morning, I rang Laura's hotel. There was no answer. After a moment's pause, I called John Ashley's. He picked up the phone.

"Yes, she's here," he said cheerily.

"How about one o'clock for lunch at the UN?" said Laura. "We'll have a couple of hours."

"Fine," I answered. Laura's cheerful voice was not able to dispel my somber mood.

Lunch passed in a depressing silence. Laura was making small talk over a baked apple topped with whipped cream. Morosely, I dug a hole in my caramel custard. Finally, I couldn't hold in my feelings any longer.

"Laurie," I said haltingly, "what will we do about the book?" Laura's face suddenly became hard.

"Would you live with me?" she asked. I was thunderstruck. The question had come at me totally out of the blue. "Laurie," I stammered, "I am married."

"I know you are married," Laura said sharply. "What I mean is, would you divorce your wife and marry me?"

"No, Laurie," I said after a lengthy pause, "I wouldn't."

"Then don't make faces like a jealous lover," Laura said furiously. "Sometimes, I think you care more about your book than about me."

Silently, I looked down into my custard. Laura had hit a raw nerve.

"Don't worry," she said with a faint trace of contempt, "before I leave, I will give you another advance of thirty thousand dollars." I raised my hand in protest. "I never want you to doubt my word again," Laura said imperiously. She was almost shouting now and several people had begun to look at our table. "Come to the bank with me," she suddenly commanded and got up from the table.

"Laurie," I said, following her down the stairs, "I can never pay you back eighty thousand dollars unless—"

"Unless the RCA book contract comes through." Laura had completed the sentence for me. "I know," she said, "and that's why you will now believe me." Ashamed that she had read my thoughts, I walked next to her in silence. I was about to hail a cab when suddenly she clutched my arm. I felt her fingernails dig into my flesh like talons. I turned and noticed that Laura's face was contorted with anger.

"You better believe me," she hissed under her breath.

"Of course I believe you, Laura," I said, frightened by her outburst.

"I will keep my promises," Laura said a bit more calmly.

"I have never doubted it," I lied, as we got into the cab.

John Ashley was waiting at the bank. "Hi," he said to me, "how is the UN?"

"Fine," I answered, mildly annoyed to see him there. Laura went to the rear of the bank and was waving to John Ashley to join her there. I sat down in the vestibule. Even though I didn't need the money, I had just about decided to accept the thirty thousand dollars. An advance of eighty thousand, I believed, would make it impossible for RCA to back out of its commitment. Besides, if Laura advanced her personal funds, she would make sure to see the project through. As I was turning over these thoughts in my mind, Laura walked up and handed me a sealed envelope. I noticed that it had a flower printed on the back.

"Meet me at my hotel in half an hour," Laura said quickly. For some reason, she seemed in a hurry to get rid of me.

"Okay," I said and took the envelope. What is John Ashley doing at the bank? I thought vaguely to myself as I walked out the door. On the way to Laura's hotel, I opened the little envelope. Inside it was a cashier's check made out to me for thirty thousand dollars.

"I have to be at the airport soon," Laura said breathlessly. She was sitting among her open suitcases and was scribbling something on a piece of paper. "Please sign it," she said to me in a brisk tone that sounded almost businesslike. The paper was another IOU. As I signed, I noticed a notation in the lower left-hand corner: "This note is cancelled in the event of my death."

"I have made the same notation on the other IOU," Laura said. "After all, I fly a great deal and one of these days I am bound to crash." Her face looked suddenly hard and bitter. "You had better take me to the airport." I looked at her. "There is no time," Laura said, reading the question in my eyes. I felt a sudden stab of pain that was so sharp it made me gasp. It was the first time that Laura had refused me. "My plane leaves in less than three hours," Laura said, in a voice that sounded a bit less harsh. Apparently, she had read my mind again. I felt a little better. Yet, I was unable to dismiss the nagging thought that a year ago, she would have found the time. Somehow, I felt vaguely that I had made a terrible mistake. Confused and with a heavy heart, I called a cab.

John Ashley was waiting at the airport. He looked tanned and fit and was wearing a sportshirt with the sleeves rolled up to his elbows. I noticed that he had powerful athletic arms. Watching him check Laura's luggage only deepened my black mood. John Ashley ordered a scotch for himself at the bar and another for Laura.

"What's yours?" he called over to me.

"An orange juice," I said ostentatiously. It was a signal to Laura of our intimacy. It did not register. Laura downed her scotch in one quick gulp and exhaled noisily. My malaise deepened into a depression.

"Time to get on board," said John Ashley.

"Right," said Laura, rising briskly from her seat. "I'll be in touch with you from London," she said to me and pecked me on the cheek.

"Laurie—" I said tentatively.

"I hate goodbyes," Laura interrupted me. "I told you that once before. Let's go quickly," she said to John Ashley, "or they will close the door."

Spring and summer came and went and I heard less and less from Laura. She would call occasionally from Africa or from the Arab Middle East, usually to ask for yet another letter. The conversations were perfunctory and brief and Laura sounded increasingly like a stranger. Instead of exhilarating me, as in the past, each conversation left me in a vague depression. In an effort to dispel my deepening malaise, I went into commodities again. For some reason, I was determined to lose Laura's thirty thousand dollars as fast as possible. My rationalization was that I could afford to lose the money since ten times that amount would soon materialize from RCA. On a deeper level, though, the money had become a symbol of my guilt, a nagging feeling that I was using Laura as a vehicle to fame and power. In my self-destructive mood, I did the exact opposite of what my brokers urged. I was advised to buy silver futures and went short; I was told that gold would triple in price and promptly sold some contracts short. To my amazement, I turned out to be right on both these moves and soon tripled my investment.

Both my brokers spoke to me in awe and praised my acumen and courage. The time had obviously come to short the market, they declared. The next candidate, in their opinion, was soybeans. I was urged to go short immediately, prices were about to fall precipitously. This time I went along and went short a huge amount of beans. Hardly had I done so when, as if on some satanic signal, prices began to rise in a steep, almost uninterrupted climb. Four weeks later, after paying up four margin calls, I was almost totally wiped out. When my broker called in his usual sepulchral tone when things went badly, I wasn't even angry. In fact, I was relieved, almost as if justice had been done.

One day in the early fall, the phone rang in my office.

"A call from Brazzaville," the operator said.

"You mean the Congo?" I asked, a little startled.

"That's right," the UN operator said. "We don't often get calls from there."

"I think I finally made it," Laura said breathlessly. Her voice sounded cheerful and her laugh was silvery again. "I can be of great service to this country," she announced, "but I need an introduction to the president."

"Are you coming to New York?" I asked, cheered up by her voice. "I might be able to introduce you to the UN ambassador to the Congo."

"That would be terrific," Laura said cheerily. "I think your problems with the institute are over."

"When are you coming?" I asked.

"I'll pass through New York for a few hours next week," Laura said. "Try to get me an appointment."

"Okay," I said. My mood had darkened once again. Laura seemed to sense it half a world away.

"I am trying to arrange for some students here to attend your university with full scholarships," she said.

"That's fine," I answered. It wasn't fine. What I needed, I noticed to my horror, was not students with full scholarships, but some kind of proof that she still cared.

The Congolese ambassador was a dignified man who, from time to time, attended my seminars at the university. He had studied at the Sorbonne, had absorbed its intellectual atmosphere, and was an ardent defender of the independence of his little country in the heart of Africa. "Rather poor and free," he liked to say, "than rich and living in servitude." When I asked him whether I could introduce an international financier to him, he smiled politely and agreed immediately.

"Bring him to my office whenever you wish," he said.

"It's a lady, Mr. Ambassador," I corrected him.

"All the better," he said diplomatically.

Two days later, Laura called from Cairo.

"I have made an appointment for you," I reported.

"That's great," she said, "do you think you could go with me to Brazzaville?" The question came as a surprise.

"I would have to think it over, Laurie," I replied evasively. "Classes have just started at the university, it would be difficult to leave."

"I'll be in New York tomorrow morning," Laura said. "You can let me know when you meet me at the airport."

The next morning Laura smiled and put her arms around me. She had gained some weight and looked a little older. I kissed her tentatively on the cheek. With a pang, I registered that she had not offered me her mouth.

"I must leave for Paris tonight at seven," she said drily, "so I had better check my luggage here. Are we seeing the Congolese ambassador?"

I nodded and took her arm. "At eleven o'clock," I said.

As we left the airport and were passing the International Hotel, I looked at Laura and squeezed her hand.

"You will have to translate for me," Laura said without expression, "I don't speak any French."

"Mr. Ambassador," Laura began, "your government is trying to borrow one hundred million dollars." The ambassador smiled politely. "I have assembled a consortium of banks that are willing to arrange the loan, but I have to get authorization from your president."

"If the professor here is willing to vouch for you," the ambassador replied after having listened to my translation, "I will give you a visa to my country and a letter to my president."

"I am giving Mademoiselle Larrabee a strong letter of my own, sir," I interjected.

"That's good enough for me," the ambassador replied. "We are a poor country and I know that we have difficulty borrowing money from the big banks." He paused and turned his head in my direction. "But I know that you, professor, have a warm spot in your heart for the small and poor. You impressed me favorably in your seminars." The ambassador had risen from his chair. "A friend of yours is a friend of mine and of my country," he said to me. "It will be a privilege to give Mademoiselle the document that you request." He made a courtly gesture. "Would you and Mademoiselle be my guests for lunch?"

Laura and I were in a taxi on our way to Kennedy. It was four o'clock in the afternoon and all the documents she needed were in order.

"I never thought you would come with me to Africa," Laura said sharply.

"Laurie," I explained, "the United States doesn't even have diplomatic relations with Congo, Brazzaville."

Laura looked at me with undisguised contempt. "I am not

afraid to go," she said. "I fly all over the world while you sit in your air-conditioned office."

I said nothing. It was true, I had decided not to go with her, but for a different reason. When I had mentioned the possibility to Caroline, she had become furious. I was simply not prepared to risk my marriage for an unpredictable safari into the heart of Africa.

"I will keep my promises to you," Laura said harshly. "I will give you the money for your institute and I will make your book a best seller, but I no longer love you."

"What have I done, Laurie?" I asked sheepishly.

"You don't love me," Laura said simply. "What you love is your ambition."

"But look what I've just done for you," I protested weakly.

Laura did not reply, but only looked at me. Her eyes had become cold and hard. "There was a time when I loved you more than life itself," she said. "I would have done anything for you, even changed my life for you."

"What do you mean, Laurie?" I asked, suddenly overcome by fear.

"It doesn't matter now, it's much too late," Laura said and laughed. It was a laugh that I had never heard before—bitter, guttural, and low. I looked at Laura with dread, remembering that other laughter, spun of silver. Her eyes stared back at me as if I were a stranger. I began to tremble.

"Laurie," I said, reaching for her hand in one last effort, "I do care for you." There was a long pause. Then Laura withdrew her hand.

"You have what you want," she said, "and so do I." We had reached the airport. "Don't come in with me," she said. "You know I hate goodbyes."

I bent over to kiss her face but drew back in horror. I had looked into her eyes: They had become glacial.

Chapter Ten

About ten weeks after Laura had left town, I received a call from John Ashley. He was in the city for a day or two, he said, and would like to see me.

"Come on over for a cup of tea," I said, "or perhaps a drink." John Ashley laughed.

"That's right, you don't drink," he said. "I'll see you at the UN this afternoon."

Despite my jealousy of John Ashley, I was pleased that he had called. Perhaps he had some news for me from Laura.

I had had only two calls from Laura since she had left, both from a hotel in London. She had reported briefly that she had been to Brazzaville, that negotiations were progressing well, and that she was hopeful that the loan transaction would be consummated shortly before Christmas. Each time I was desperate to ask about the book, but was afraid of annoying her. Instead, I called Bernard Hewitt who said that he hadn't heard from Laura for quite some time. On one occasion, I called Mr. Sarnoff's office. A secretary came on the line.

"Mr. Sarnoff is in conference," she said in a metallic voice, "may I take a message?"

"No, thank you," I replied after I had identified myself. "I would like to speak to him in person."

"We'll have to call you back," the secretary said.

After waiting for two days, I decided to telephone again. "He has stepped out of the office," the metallic voice said cheerily. Why do all New York secretaries use the same old tired phrases? I thought to myself as I hung up the telephone.

I tried twice more that afternoon, but couldn't reach the RCA executive. He was in a meeting, the robot lady said, and couldn't be disturbed. Clearly, Mr. Sarnoff did not know who I was and did not wish to speak to me.

At five o'clock, John Ashley appeared with an elderly gentleman.

"This is a lawyer friend of mine, Mr. Laughton," John Ashley said. My secretary served tea to the three of us and left the room. There was an awkward silence. Suddenly, I had the feeling that this was no mere social call.

"Have you heard from Laura?" John Ashley asked.

"She called me a couple of weeks ago," I reported truthfully.

"Where is she now?" asked John Ashley.

"The last time I spoke to her she was in London," I replied. "When did you see her last?" I asked.

John Ashley didn't answer.

"The last time Mr. Ashley saw Miss Larrabee was four months ago," interjected Mr. Laughton.

"She has disappeared," added John Ashley.

A cold fear had begun to crawl up my spine.

"What can I do for you?" I asked.

"Before she disappeared, Laura told me that she gave you thirty thousand dollars of my money," Ashley said. "Is that correct?"

The teacup I was holding in my hand trembled violently. Ashley's presence at the bank had suddenly flashed through my mind. "Laura loaned me that amount as an advance against my book," I said.

"When?" Mr. Laughton asked sharply.

"In the middle of March 1973," I replied. The two men exchanged a glance.

"You've got thirty thousand dollars of my money," John Ashley said. Suddenly, I felt my anger rise.

"I signed a note to Laura for the money," I replied.

"I don't care what you two did," John Ashley said. His ruddy face had become flushed. "I want my money back."

My own pulse had begun to beat rapidly. My fear had left me and was replaced by a growing fury. Of what was he accusing me?

"I don't owe you any money, John," I declared. "I owe the money to Laura. And, by the way, do you have a note from her? Why did you give her the money?"

John Ashley looked at me. I noticed that small beads of perspiration had formed on his forehead. "You mean you don't know?" he asked sarcastically.

"Of course not," I replied.

"The funds were to block a two-million-dollar loan for Mr. Ashley in a bank in Switzerland," Mr. Laughton interjected.

"And did you get the loan?" I asked.

"I didn't get the loan and she has disappeared with every cent I've got!"

"How much, for God's sake?" I choked out, my throat constricting.

"Sixty thousand dollars," John Ashley said.

I had put the teacup on the little table, trying to appear calm and in control of my emotions.

"Do you mean to tell me," I said hoarsely, "that Laura stole sixty thousand dollars of your money and gave me half of it?"

"That's exactly right," said John Ashley. "I don't want to

make any trouble, but I want my money back. If you know where she is, you'd better get in touch with her."

By now I was shaking and my mind was reeling. It took me a few seconds to regain my composure. The two men were staring at me suspiciously.

"I'll try to call Laura tomorrow and have her call you," I said weakly.

"Fine," said John Ashley, rising from his chair. "I am on my way back to Toronto in an hour. I'll give you a week. After that I plan to go to the Canadian authorities."

Numb with shock, I stared at the two men as they walked out the door. Alone in my office, I slumped in my chair. Unable to move, I sat crouched over my desk for half an hour. Suddenly, it occurred to me that I should have given John Ashley the number of Laura's hotel in London. I had no way of reaching him now. Frantic with anxiety, I had to do something to relieve my tension. I picked up the phone and gave the operator Laura's number. "It's after midnight in London," the operator said. "I know that, please connect me anyway," I replied.

"What is it?" Laura said sleepily. Her voice sounded irritated.

"Laurie," I said, my heart pounding in my throat, "John Ashley came to see me with a lawyer today; he told me that you gave me thirty thousand dollars of his money. Is that true?" There was a pause at the other end.

"What else did he say?" asked Laura. Her voice suddenly was alert and cold.

"He wants his money back," I said. "He wants sixty thousand dollars or he will complain to the Canadian authorities."

"Let him complain," Laura interrupted me. "He is a crook and I am taking him to court."

"Laurie," I pleaded, "please come back and straighten out this mess; he wants the money back from *me*." The phone slipped from my sweaty palm and fell to the floor.

"You don't owe him any money, you signed a note to me," Laura said. Her voice had become strident. "This is between him and me. Why don't you stay out of it?"

"I would love to," I croaked in a failed attempt at laughter, "but I don't believe that he will let me."

"I will take care of it," said Laura. Her voice had suddenly become calm.

"Please do," I begged, "I can't pay the money twice, once to you and once to him."

"I'll call him in Toronto," Laura repeated, her voice rising.

"Can't you come back and settle it in person?" I asked.

"I am in the middle here. I have more important things to do," Laura said, "and now please let me get back to sleep."

"Laurie!" I shouted across the transatlantic wire. Then I heard a click. Laura had disconnected.

I couldn't sleep that night. At 4:00 A.M., I called Laura again in London. Surely, I thought, she would be up by ten. A clerk came on the line.

"Miss Larrabee has checked out," he said laconically.

"Where to?" I asked, my heart sinking.

"She's left no forwarding address," said the clerk and hung up the phone. Four hours later, I called John Ashley's number in Toronto.

"Has she called yet?" I asked frantically.

"You should know," said John Ashley.

"No, I don't," I said weakly. This time, my fear was greater than my fury.

"You've got three days," he now said.

A few days before Christmas, my secretary knocked at the door. "There is someone on the phone who wants urgently to speak with you," she said. I picked up the telephone.

"This is Inspector Kraft of the United States Postal Service," said a flat, hard voice.

"Postal Service?" I repeated, uncomprehendingly.

"I would like to see you," said the voice.

"May I ask what this is all about?" I asked politely.

"There is a criminal investigation in progress," said the voice.

"A criminal investigation?" I repeated mechanically. My entire body had begun to tremble. "About whom?" I asked.

"About Miss Larrabee and about you," answered the cold, flat voice.

"I am Inspector Kraft and this is Inspector Slade." Each man handed me a card. They were medium-size nondescript individuals in their middle thirties.

"Nice view you have from here, professor," said Kraft, looking out the window of my UN office.

"What can I do for you, inspector?" I asked, refusing to be drawn into preliminary pleasantries.

"Do you know Miss Laura Larrabee?" Kraft asked.

"Yes," I replied.

"Did you write this letter for her?" Kraft placed before me a copy of the letter I had written on Laura's behalf to the Viennese bank almost two years before.

"How did you get hold of that?" I asked, surprised.

"It's up to us to ask the questions," Kraft said coldly.

"I am sorry," I said, intimidated.

"Why did you write it?" asked Slade.

"She promised to raise money for an academic pet project of mine," I replied.

"How well do you know her?" Slade asked.

"Quite well, I think," I said.

"On what basis did you write this sentence? 'Miss Laura Larrabee has an impeccable reputation and has closed numerous financial transactions to the satisfaction of both borrower and lender,' " Kraft read in a monotone.

I had broken out in a sweat. "I know her well," I stammered finally.

"Do you know of any transaction that she actually closed?" Slade asked.

I shook my head.

"Do you know any lender?"

"No," I said.

"Or any borrower?"

Again, I shook my head. "I simply took her word for it," I said. There was a pause.

"Do you have an intimate relationship with her?" asked Kraft.

I nodded again.

By now I was so terrified that I was unable to speak. There was another pause. The two men glanced at one another.

"Do you know John Ashley?" Slade asked sharply.

"Yes," I nodded.

"Did Miss Larrabee ever give you any money?" asked Kraft.

"No," I lied, completely panicked. I was about to add: She loaned me the money, but my terror and humiliation prevented me from making the correction. I kept silent, hoping that Kraft wouldn't ask whether Laura had given me a loan. He didn't. The two men rose, their faces totally without expression. I felt that, somehow, I had made a catastrophic blunder, but I seemed unable to admit it.

"That's all the questions we've got," Kraft said in his flat voice. "Goodbye."

During the night, I was unable to sleep. While technically I had told the truth, I knew that I had actually lied. By daybreak, I knew that I would have to call Kraft back. At nine o'clock, I dialed his number.

"Inspector," I began in a voice that I hoped was casual, "I would like to make a correction."

"What is it?" Kraft asked gruffly. I took a deep breath to calm my terror.

"Miss Larabee loaned me thirty thousand dollars last March." I wanted to go on and tell him about the earlier loan as well but Kraft interrupted.

"We know all about it," he said coldly, "including the bank on which the check was drawn." My mouth went dry again. "You have lied to a federal officer," Kraft said. "That is a serious crime."

"I didn't lie," I managed to croak into the phone. "I didn't lie," I repeated desperately.

"Come in to see me the day after New Year's," Kraft said and hung up the phone.

"It would be better for you if you confessed," Kraft said. I was sitting in his office on the top floor of the General Post Office. For three days and nights I had called hotels all over Europe trying to reach Laura. She was nowhere to be found. Caroline, concerned about my state of mind and about the investigation, had begged me to consult a lawyer. Paralyzed with fear, I found myself unable to take action. "I have nothing to fear from the inspector," I told Caroline, "I don't need a lawyer."

"You might as well confess," Kraft said. Numb with terror, I looked at him. "You wrote phony letters for your lady friend, she used the letters to rip off John Ashley, and you split the loot fifty-fifty, isn't that correct?"

Suddenly, I felt warm liquid on the inside of my leg. I had urinated in my pants. "No, for God's sake, no," I pleaded in a voice shrill with despair. "That's not true, inspector, that's not true!"

"That's the way it looks to me," Kraft said, totally unmoved. I was bathed in perspiration.

"I never wrote a letter to John Ashley," I cried out.

"You better persuade your lady friend to come back from London," said Kraft. "I want to see the two of you together in a week."

"I will try to reach her," I said weakly.

Kraft looked at me with contempt. "You better try a little harder, then," he said. "I want you two and the money in a week from now, or I will inform the United States Attorney."

"What do you mean?" I said tonelessly.

"You will get indicted for fraud," Kraft said.

"Laura, thank God I reached you," I cried in relief. I had finally tracked Laura down in another hotel in London. "The United States government thinks we are in cahoots to defraud John Ashley," I stammered into the telephone. "I beg you to come back." There was a pause at the other end. "If you ever loved me, please come back," I begged, hanging on to the phone as if it were a lifeline.

"Meet me at Kennedy tomorrow night," Laura said after a brief pause.

"Thank you, Laurie," I said, weeping with relief. "I'll be there."

The London flight was half an hour late. I stood at the sliding doors again. The memory of a similar scene two years before flashed through my mind. A pilot walked out of the door.

"Was the plane full?" I asked.

"Almost empty," said the pilot. "Not much doing from London this time of year."

About a dozen passengers filed past me. Desperately, I searched each face. And suddenly I knew. Laura was not going to get off that plane.

"I missed the flight," Laura said on the telephone, "but I reached Kraft. I told him I was sending a courier with the funds."

"Thank you, Laurie," I said, my despair giving way to renewed hope.

"And I have even added interest," said Laura. "The man

is coming with a cashier's check for sixty-four thousand, five hundred dollars—made out to John Ashley. His name is George Watson. You can meet him tomorrow night at Kennedy."

"Same flight?" I asked.

"Same flight," said Laura.

Later, I called Kraft.

"That's right," Kraft said, "she called me too." His voice sounded a shade more friendly. "Bring the check in to me as soon as possible."

"Of course I will, inspector," I said eagerly.

This time the plane was half an hour early. Twenty passengers got off. I had George Watson paged, but no one answered to his name. Finally, in desperation, I managed to get a copy of the list of passengers. The name Watson was nowhere to be seen.

"Watson had a personal emergency," Laura said on the phone. "But I am Telexing the money bank to bank. I have already phoned Kraft."

"That's right," Kraft said, "she called me again." His voice sounded cold and threatening. "You two better stop cooking up ploys to throw me off the track." I was trembling again.

"Didn't she send a Telex?" I asked desperately.

"She sent a Telex promising that, by tomorrow, she would transmit sixty-four thousand, five hundred dollars."

"Thank God," I managed to say weakly as I hung up the phone.

Next afternoon, Kraft called. "I have not received the money," he said coldly. "The bank has not received it either."

"She told me it would be here today," I said hopelessly.

"You two seem to think I was born yesterday," Kraft said. There was a cold fury in his voice.

"Believe me, inspector—" I began.

"I am turning over the matter to the United States Attorney," Kraft interrupted. "You may expect to be sub-poenaed before a grand jury for fraud. I have nothing more to say to you."

"Laurie," I shouted desperately. It was an hour later. "You didn't send the money. I will be indicted. Kraft thinks I am a thief. I will lose my job." In my terror, I had begun to shout. "I beg you to come back, I beg you on my life."

There was silence on the other end.

"Please, Laurie," I pleaded. "Please come back." I stopped pleading and waited for her answer. I heard nothing. "Laurie," I screamed, "are you there?" Suddenly over the static, I heard laughter. It was low and guttural as if coming from the depths of hell.

"Yes, I am here," said Laura, and laughed again, "I am here."

"Laurie!" I shrieked and dropped the telephone. The receiver fell on top of a glass of water from which I had been drinking. The glass shattered. I reached for the receiver. "Laurie!" I shrieked again. "What are you saying?" My hand was bleeding heavily. I had cut myself on a piece of glass and blood was dripping on my desk.

And then I heard the laughter, low and cruel: "Yes, I am here," said Laura. "I am here, and I am going to destroy you."

"She has lied to both of us, inspector, please believe me." I had rushed to Kraft's office and was facing the inspector. "Please let me call her now in front of you," I begged, "so that you can see that I am not misleading you." Kraft looked at me appraisingly for a long moment. There had been a traffic jam and I had run the last few blocks. The sweat was pouring down my face.

"Okay, professor," he said finally, handing me the receiver, "charge it to your number."

I asked for Laura's hotel in London, with the inspector

listening in. A clerk came on the line. He sounded puzzled when I asked for Laura.

"There's no one here by that name," he said curtly in a cockney accent.

"But I spoke to her last night," I insisted, trying to maintain control over an icy, choking panic.

"She may have checked out last night," the clerk said without hesitation, "but I never heard of her."

"Well, professor?" Kraft's face was grim.

"I'd better get myself a lawyer," I said, unable to control my trembling.

"You had better," said Kraft, "because you are going before the grand jury."

"You mustn't pay Ashley any money," said Bernice Lerner, an attorney. "You don't owe him any, you owe it to Laura Larrabee. It would be double liability for you."

I shook my head. "The money doesn't matter," I said. "It's the investigation that will kill me."

"Paying the money to John Ashley wouldn't stop the investigation," countered Mrs. Lerner. "Once the machine begins to grind, it goes on grinding." I looked at her in consternation. "Besides," added Mrs. Lerner, "if you offered to pay Ashley money, it would look like an admission of guilt."

"Damned if I do and damned if I don't," I whispered desperately.

"They will subpoena you before a grand jury," Mrs. Lerner said after a pause, "and you had better get ready."

"How?" I asked.

"We know now," said Mrs. Lerner, "where the thirty thousand came from. What about the fifty thousand?"

"I have no idea," I said truthfully, a new shock wave going through my body.

"You'd better start thinking," Mrs. Lerner said.

Bernice Lerner was a competent attorney who had helped me in a couple of legal matters. Her mind was orderly and logical and I had finally decided to tell her about Laura Larrabee, even though she had little experience in criminal law. "Write up the facts," she had told me crisply. When she had read the more than fifty pages I had written, she took off her glasses and looked me in the face.

"I see no criminal liability on your part," she said slowly, "but I can see how it appears to the inspector."

"What do you mean?" I asked although I already knew the answer.

"You wrote letters and you got money," Mrs. Lerner said simply. "Laura probably showed your 'To Whom It May Concern' letters to John Ashley; and then she split the money with you fifty-fifty."

"Thirty-thirty," I corrected her in an unsuccessful try at humor. Mrs. Lerner didn't laugh.

"You may have to take a lie detector test," she said.

"Absolutely," I said eagerly. "When?"

"We will have to think about it," said Mrs. Lerner. "It's not so simple."

I rushed back home and looked for the monthly statements of my bank account over which Laura had power of attorney. They were lying in a bottom drawer where I had thrown them carelessly. I hadn't even opened them. Now I went through them carefully, hoping for a clue to the fifty-thousand-dollar loan. After a brief search, I found a cancelled check for fifteen hundred dollars made out to a North Dakota bank, dated a month after Laura had given me the loan. The memo on the cancelled check said "interest on loan." I brought the check to Mrs. Lerner, who examined it thoughtfully on both sides.

"You may have something there," she said. "Call me tomorrow."

She called me back an hour later.

"I've called North Dakota," she said. "Your friend Laura Larrabee ripped off the bank for two hundred thousand dollars." I sat crumpled in my chair.

"How?" I managed to croak into the telephone.

"A fraudulent loan with phony stock," said Mrs. Lerner. Two days later, at the office, I received a call from the Congolese ambassador. Could you come over this afternoon? he asked; it was an urgent matter. I noted with anxiety that the ambassador was direct and to the point. There was a total absence of the usual diplomatic niceties when he asked me to see him in his office. He said that he would be alone.

"Professor, I must say that I am shocked," the ambassador said in his most polished French. I looked at him, bracing myself for yet another blow. "Mademoiselle Larrabee has disappeared," the ambassador began. I nodded, slightly relieved.

"I know," I said, twisting my face into the grimace of a smile, "I don't know where she is either."

"You don't understand, professor," the ambassador insisted. I looked at him, my smile vanishing. "She tried to rob my country of a million dollars," the ambassador continued. My mouth fell open but there was no sound. The ambassador rose from his chair, his eyes burning with anger. "She told our president that she had arranged a loan for our country, but that she needed her commission first before she would deliver the funds." The ambassador was breathing heavily. "We trusted her, or rather we trusted you, so we gave her a cashier's check for a million dollars. Fortunately, our finance minister decided to telephone the lending bank in France before mademoiselle left the country." The ambassador had begun to pace up and down in front of me. "Our minister wanted to thank the banker, who was an old school friend from the Sorbonne. 'What loan, what Mademoiselle Larrabee?' asked the banker." The ambassador's voice had risen to a shout. His eyes had begun to roll in his head with rage. "We threw her out of the country," he said, a bit more calmly. "Out of courtesy to you, professor, we didn't throw her into jail." I looked at the ambassador. The tears welled up inside me.

"I wish you had," I said. "I wish you had."

I walked into the grand jury room. I hadn't slept the night before and had just vomited in the adjoining men's room. Mrs. Lerner, who had to wait outside, had given me a last encouraging smile. The room was sparse and bleak. I noticed three ascending tiers of about twenty seats, occupied by men and women who were bantering and joking with each other. When they saw me enter, they suddenly fell silent. For some reason, I thought of a subway train. The twenty people looked exactly like a cross section of rush-hour subway riders. Seated at the table was a young prosecutor with a prematurely balding head who was riffling busily through a sheaf of documents.

"Do you swear to tell the truth, the whole truth, and nothing but the truth?" the foreman asked.

"I do," I answered and sat down.

I glanced at the men and women of the jury. They were looking at me curiously like an animal in a zoo. I took out my handkerchief and wiped my face. I heard a jury member whisper something to another. Suddenly, I knew that no matter what I said, no one would believe me. The reason, I noticed to my horror, was not because I was about to lie or that I had a crime to hide. It was because I felt consumed by a guilt that was so profound that it was paralyzing me.

It's about time you landed here, a voice inside me said. The prosecutor's balding head reminded me of Oscar. You will end up in the gutter as a criminal, said Oscar's voice inside me.

I was answering the prosecutor's questions. I answered truthfully, but I felt guilty just the same. The men and women on my left seemed to look more and more hostile with each question. The prosecutor placed letters and documents in front of me. I answered his questions more and more mechanically. For some reason, Eddie and my father's cemetery kept intruding in my mind. Part of me seemed to have split off from the rest. Finally, after what seemed an interminable time, the prosecutor said: "I have no more questions, you are discharged subject to recall."

Outside, Mrs. Lerner was waiting.

"How was it?" she asked sympathetically. I looked at her.

"I learned something today," I answered. "It is more difficult to be innocent than to be guilty."

"What do you mean?" asked Mrs. Lerner.

"No one believes me," I said desperately. "If I were really guilty of conspiracy and fraud, I would have confessed long ago. But this is a special kind of hell." Mrs. Lerner nodded. "I almost wish I were guilty," I said quietly.

I went before the grand jury twice more. I had become suicidal and was seeing a psychiatrist every day. My contract at the United Nations was not renewed. No one told me why but I suspected that it was because of Laura Larrabee. After seven years of service, I resigned.

Caroline had become terrified that I would take my life. One morning, she put her arms around me and said softly: "I need you more than ever now." I came out of my fog and looked at her. "We'll have a baby," she said.

Mrs. Lerner tried to cheer me up. "They will not indict you," she kept saying.

"Why not?" I asked.

"Because Laura Larrabee has disappeared," she said, "and they are not going to bring you to trial without her."

Our child was born during a heavy snowstorm.

"What shall we call her?" I asked Caroline.

"I love the name Anna," said my wife.

"How about Anna Elizabeth?" I said. Caroline reached for my hand.

"Don't worry," she said, "they will never catch her; she's probably married some wealthy sheik by now and has a wig and a new name." Gratefully, I smiled down at my wife.

"I hope you're right," I said, "I hope you're right."

Chapter Eleven

The birth of our daughter in early 1975 was like an omen of good fortune. My final traumatic conversation with Laura had become a distant memory. As an extra precautionary measure, I had finally retained the counsel of a brilliant lawyer who had served as chief of the criminal division in the Department of Justice. Despite his relative youth, at 42 Harold had great maturity. He was careful and deliberate, and had a way of qualifying his assertions with numerous subordinate clauses. When he declared on one occasion that the Larrabee file was no doubt buried at the bottom of some remote government filing cabinet, I finally dismissed the entire affair as a nightmare.

"A danger would arise," Harold said, "only if she were to return to the United States, and she would have to be crazy to do that!"

Caroline and I gradually developed a genuine affection for Harold. After a few months, we forgot that he was my lawyer. He had become a family friend.

My personal life during that time became happier than I had ever dared to hope. Caroline and I experienced a new sense of intimacy and sharing. We regarded our little daughter as a blessing that had come our way relatively late in life. Caroline turned out to be a loving and devoted mother. Her artistic career, too, had begun to blossom. With joy and pride I listened to her perform Beethoven's Fourth Piano Concerto in a sensitive and moving reading.

After many years of separation, my son had reentered my life. Richard had become a handsome, serious young man. Caroline and I became involved in his life and when the time came for him to apply to colleges, we were able to be helpful with advice. Richard was admitted to a fine university in the Boston area. He was on his way. My son and I were eventually able to talk openly about the past. I felt proud and happy when he introduced me to his fellow students as his father.

My boyhood friend, Rusty, also reentered my life. It had always been his hope to visit the United States. He wrote that he had found an excellent position in a textile firm in North Carolina. Two months later, I met him at the airport in New York. We embraced and almost thirty years of separation fell away. We told each other that we hadn't changed and laughed. It was a lie, of course, yet on another level it was true. We had never ceased to love each other.

I also had the opportunity to reactivate my old friendship with Henry Kissinger. During that painful spring of 1975 when diplomatic relations between him and the Israeli leadership had reached an all-time low, I would visit Henry in his office at the State Department and talk about the Middle East. On one such occasion, Henry was terribly depressed. It was the day on which Saigon had fallen, Portugal and Cyprus were in turmoil, and the Watergate disaster was an all too recent memory. But what affected Henry most was the attitude of many Jewish leaders in America who were openly attacking him.

"I am a Jew, too," he said with a deep sadness. "How can they believe that I would ever betray my own people?"

In early 1976, we invited Hans Morgenthau for a birthday dinner. Henry had agreed to come to honor his old mentor. The Secret Service had come to check out the apartment. Word had gotten out and a crowd had gathered at the entrance of the apartment house to catch a glimpse of our illustrious dinner guest. Henry flew in from Washington despite a snowstorm. Though the two men had been intellectual adversaries, especially over Vietnam and the Middle East, they had retained a genuine respect and affection for each other. Henry was in an expansive mood and reminisced about his conversations with Chou En-lai and Mao Tse-tung in China. As my friends sat down at our dinner table enjoying Caroline's superb cuisine, I experienced a moment of undiluted joy. I looked at my wife, at Henry, and at Hans Morgenthau and raised my glass.

"To many more such birthdays in good health for all of us," I said.

My professional life, too, was beginning to give me a new sense of satisfaction. I had published a new study about war and was hard at work on a book about Henry's foreign policy. If ever in my life I felt a sense of stability and balance, it was during that brief spring of 1976. Little Anna had begun to string together her first words. "Papa," she would say, and smile at me.

And then, one day, the telephone rang. I was sitting at my desk, working on my manuscript. It was Harold.

"I'm afraid I have bad news for you," he said. "They have arrested Laura Larrabee."

I felt nothing. It was as if I had always known that I was living on borrowed time.

"Where?" I asked, as if it mattered.

"In Miami," Harold said. "She tried to enter the United States under the name of her Arab husband."

"They are going to indict you for conspiracy and fraud," said Harold. I was sitting in his office. Somehow I felt that this was not really happening to me, that I was in the midst of a horrendous nightmare from which I would awake at any moment.

"But I am innocent," I said. Unable to think, I had repeated the same phrase probably six or seven times.

"Irving Katz does not believe you," Harold said. "He thinks you wrote phony letters deliberately in order to share in Laura Larrabee's ill-gotten gains."

"Who is Irving Katz?" I asked.

"He is a young prosecutor in his twenties who was assigned the Larrabee case. He would love to put you behind bars for many years." I sank back in my chair. "But we have a chance—a slim one, but in my view, worth taking," Harold said, his eyes focused on my face. "Katz will let you take a lie detector test." It took me a moment to register Harold's words. Then a tremendous wave of relief swept over me.

"Thank God," I said. "If the machine will do what it is supposed to do, it will exonerate me."

"If you pass," Harold stated sternly, "Katz will give you immunity from prosecution. But if you flunk, he will not only indict you, but we will have to consent to the use of the test results at your trial."

"In other words, if I fail the test," I said, "I will be convicted and I will go to jail."

"That's a fair interpretation," Harold said.

"I'll take the test," I said.

My relationship to machines had never been a good one. Even as a boy, I had shied away from them. The fact that a machine would now decide my fate filled me with foreboding. Yet, the alternative seemed worse. The only thing that reassured me was that the truth was on my side. Harold and Irving Katz bargained for another week over the person who was to administer the test. Finally they reached an agreement. I was to appear the following day in the office of a Mr. Clarke who was head of a concern that described itself as the Lie Detection Service. The night before the test I had an attack of such primordial terror that Caroline literally sat on top of me to stop me from injuring myself. When dawn finally came, after that endless night, I was drenched in death sweat.

Mr. Clarke was a wiry little man who tried his best to put me at my ease. He was a retired army officer with an office full of mementos of a military life.

"Let's first go over the questions the government has given me," he said. "I do that with every testee."

There were about twenty questions that covered the story fairly completely. Only one, I realized immediately, was crucial. "Did you know, when you received the funds from Laura Larrabee, that they were the proceeds of a fraud?" Mr. Clarke spent an inordinate amount of time discussing that question. My answer was always the same: "No, I didn't know. I only found out many months later." Finally, when he asked me the same question for the sixth or seventh time, apparently to emphasize its crucial importance, I blurted out, "Mr. Clarke, please believe me, I'm innocent." Suddenly, the little man's eyes narrowed into two suspicious slits. "That won't do you any good here, Doctor," he said. "I let my machine do my thinking for me."

Mr. Clarke harnessed me into a number of mechanical contraptions. He tied a kind of belt around my chest to monitor my breathing. A tight band was wrapped around my upper arm to measure blood pressure. Finally, a piece of metal was attached to my index finger to measure the rate of perspiration. While he attached these infernal instruments, Mr. Clarke explained their significance in a detached and businesslike manner.

"Don't worry, I won't hurt you," he said finally, before he switched on his machines and began the test.

The crucial question was placed somewhere in the middle of the lot. Slowly, I felt my pressure rising as Mr. Clarke asked a bunch of innocuous questions about my age and

background. It rose, I realized in desperation, not because
I was about to lie, but because I understood the importance
of the question and my terror was rising in anticipation. I
begged my body to remain calm but it refused to cooperate.
Perversely, it had become my adversary. When Clarke
asked the question on which my fate depended, my anxiety
shot up so sharply that it probably set a new record for
mendacity. Suddenly, out of nowhere, Oscar's voice flashed
through my mind: You will end up in the gutter as a criminal. My pressure went down again as Mr. Clarke continued
questioning me. At the very end, he asked a question for
which he had not prepared me.

"I will now ask you something very personal," he said.

"Fine," I answered, completely calmed by resignation.

"Actually, I won't ask it," Mr. Clarke said a moment
later with a laugh. "That was a control question. Most people think I am about to ask about their sex life and their
anxiety shoots up because they are about to lie."

Suddenly, I realized that this little man was stupid. Not
evil or malevolent, but merely stupid beyond hope. His
primitive machine, I now realized with black despair, had
wrecked my life. My blood pressure had shot up when it
should have remained low and had remained low when it
should have spurted up. Heavily, without a word, I rose
from Mr. Clarke's lie-detection chair. Appeals to him, I
knew, were useless.

"I'll inform your attorney and Mr. Katz about the results," he said with an air of self-importance.

It was clear that his machine was Mr. Clarke's religion. I
thought of Eddie and my father in the little cemetery in
Vienna as I walked out the door.

"You failed the test and Katz will surely now indict you,"
Harold said. His voice on the phone, full of concern, seemed
to come from a great distance. The news gave me a kind of

perverse pleasure. I had accurately predicted the results of
Mr. Clarke's machine.

"So what happens now?" I asked with almost masochistic
curiosity.

"We have one more chance," Harold said. "I have persuaded Katz that he should meet with you. He will question
you about the case."

"What's the purpose of this horrible game?" I blurted out.

"He wants to consider you as a potential government witness against Laura Larrabee at her forthcoming trial."

"When is her trial?" I interrupted Harold. My lawyer
ignored the question.

"If you can persuade Katz that you would make a cred-
ible witness on the stand, and his case against Laura needs
your help, he may agree to let you plead guilty to a lesser
charge than conspiracy and fraud."

"But I am not guilty of anything," I cried out.

"I don't believe you are guilty of conspiracy and fraud
either," Harold answered. "But you did lie to that federal
inspector and you did write some letters you should not
have written. My partner David and I are doing some research to see if there is a lesser and different offense to which
you could quite fairly plead guilty. Is that clear?"

My head was in a whirl while Harold spoke, but when I
forced myself to think, I realized that it was all too clear.
Deep in my heart, I had known that Laura was not honest,
had lied to me, and had used my emotional involvement to
further her own ends. "When do we meet with him?"
I asked Harold.

"Tonight at seven o'clock," he said.

At six o'clock, I picked up Harold at his office. He had
asked his partner David to come along. David was a prematurely balding man in his early thirties who had occasionally sat in on our conversations. He had a razor-sharp
intelligence and an uncanny ability to grasp complex material in an amazingly short period of time. Though he was

basically kind and had sincerely wished me luck before my fateful appointment with Mr. Clarke's machine, David was not a patient man. My compulsive tendency, in my despair, to repeat everything I told him several times exasperated him. "You have already told me that," he liked to say with a tolerant but slightly irritated smile.

The meeting was to take place in a windowless room that already reeked of stale cigarette smoke and sweat. Katz and another young assistant United States Attorney entered, carrying several heavy folders. They were accompanied by an elderly postal inspector whom I had met briefly in Kraft's office three years earlier. Nobody really said anything.

"I am hungry," Harold announced suddenly. "Let's order some food from the Chinese restaurant."

I looked at Harold in amazement. What was he doing? Katz leaned over and said, "How about some greasy eggrolls?" Everyone laughed. I realized that Harold's comment had broken the initial tension. Shortly afterward, a messenger arrived with six orders of soggy Chinese food. To my own amazement, I, too, had ordered dinner. I poked around in my egg fu yung as the lawyers ate hungrily and bantered among themselves in a spirit of informal camaraderie.

"Time to get the muggers off the streets," Harold said and laughed.

Katz had finished his chicken chow mein and was now sipping coffee from a paper cup.

"Why don't we get started, Irv," said Harold.

"Very well," said Katz, and looked at me through his thick glasses. Suddenly, I sensed a palpable electric tension.

"We have decided to indict you, Doctor, but the government is considering the possibility of using you as a witness," Katz began. I nodded. "Whether we do so or not depends upon our judgment of your credibility."

"I have every intention of telling the truth," I answered. It occurred to me that I should have gone to the men's room first. I did not want to urinate in my pants again.

As Katz began his questioning and I began to tell my tale, my terror gradually left me. The possibility of contact, the chance to tell my story to another human being, gave me hope. I looked at Irving Katz. He was young, I thought, hardly older than my students. Despite the lateness of the hour, he was dressed meticulously. His shirt collar, I noticed, was of a different color from his shirt. As the evening progressed, he took off his jacket and revealed a pair of suspenders and a disproportionately large posterior. His questions were often convoluted and when I asked him to repeat them, he would apologize profusely.

"I know, Doctor," he would say, "that you are probably a lot more intelligent than I."

At one point during the proceedings, the telephone rang. "What is the subject of your conversation?" asked Katz, who had picked up the receiver. There was a pause. "State your position," said the prosecutor in a level voice. He listened for a couple of minutes. "I have no objections if you do and I have no objections if you don't," he then said coolly. "Fine," he concluded, "I will inform you later of my decision. Excuse me," Katz said, as he returned to the table. "That was my wife. We are trying to decide whether to go to the opera next week."

Irving Katz, I realized by midnight, was not waging a vendetta. He exuded the kind of meticulous pedantic obsession with detail that I had sometimes seen in students who had racked up straight-A records more through tenacity and diligence than through insight or imagination. Yet, Katz struck me as a man of absolute integrity to whom his work was sacrosanct. But he was, I observed with sinking heart, very, very young. And in the hands of this boy hardly older than my son, to whom each question had either a black or a white answer, lay my future. Correction, I thought to myself: This boy had not assumed that awesome power arbitrarily. I myself had given it to him.

The meeting broke up shortly after midnight. I was left alone in the dark room while the two prosecutors and my lawyers went to another office to discuss my fate. The postal inspector sat around idly for a while smoking a cigar. Then he, too, left the room.

"The legal eagles might take quite a while," he said, disappearing down the corridor.

I glanced at the table. Katz had left some papers lying there. The top folder lay open and I began to leaf through the papers mechanically. Suddenly I realized that what I was reading was a nearly final draft of an indictment against Laura Larrabee and me for conspiracy and fraud. It was about ten pages in length and presented me as the mastermind of a criminal conspiracy in the United Nations with Laura Larrabee doing the legwork for me. With curiosity, I noticed that I no longer felt any terror. The part of me that had registered pain or pleasure in the past seemed to have split off. I sat there like a stone.

"Well, you shook 'em up," said Harold, as he reentered the room. "But they still aren't totally convinced; they want another meeting tomorrow night at seven."

"With Chinese food again?" I asked in a vain attempt at humor. Harold looked at me.

"You did very well," he said sincerely. "Go on like this tomorrow night, and Katz might decide to use you as a witness and let you plead to a lesser charge."

"I am not guilty of any crime, goddamn it," I shouted suddenly. "Why don't we go to trial?"

"I have thought about that carefully," said Harold, "and I advise against it." I looked at him in consternation. "You and Laura would be tried together," Harold said. "You are obviously more educated and intelligent than she."

"I wonder," I said, smiling bitterly.

"The jury would hear about and see the letters you wrote and know that she gave you money." He paused to let his words sink in. "And then Katz would parade the failed lie detector test in front of them." I had begun to tremble. "You would probably be convicted," Harold said.

"Innocently?" I asked.

"That's right," said Harold. "We've got to try like hell to make them buy a lesser charge."

The second meeting was a rerun of the first. Katz went over the same ground again and asked the same questions in a dozen convoluted ways. When I told the story about Laura's deception with my book, I broke down in tears. Katz looked at me with an air of slight repugnance as if I were a large insect being vivisected on a laboratory table. Again, the meeting went past midnight. Again there was a conference and I was left alone in the stale air of the little room.

Half an hour later, Harold and David walked in, smiling broadly.

"We have what we wanted—no indictment for fraud," said Harold. "They want you as a witness at Laura Larrabee's trial and they have allowed you to plead guilty to a much lesser charge." I said nothing. "And there will be no publicity," Harold added, "no one will be the wiser."

Harold drove me home in silence. That night I slept after taking a large dose of Valium. The next morning I called Harold to express my gratitude. His wife, Suzanne, came on the line. Her voice sounded strained and unnatural.

"What's wrong?" I asked.

"Harold is in the hospital," she said. "You won't be able to talk to him for quite some time."

"What's wrong with him?" I shrieked in panic.

"I can't tell you that," said Harold's wife and hung up the phone.

"Harold has had a heart attack," said David. "He will be

out of the office for some time. I will now take over the case
if you want me as your lawyer."

"Of course I want you," I responded. "Was it a massive
attack?" I then asked with trepidation.

"Every heart attack is serious," David said evasively. "But
before it hit him, we were able to convince Katz to accept a
guilty plea of misprision."

"Of what?" I asked.

"Misprision," David repeated. "It means failure to report
someone else's crime."

"You are the lawyer," I said, "what happens now?"

"We go before a federal judge and make your plea and
then you will be sentenced."

"Sentenced?" I echoed fearfully.

"That's right," said David, "and there are a few things
you must do now so that I can keep you out of jail."

"When must I make this plea?" I asked.

"Tomorrow morning," David said.

The high-ceilinged courthouse chamber resounded with
the echoes of many muffled voices. About a hundred people
were sitting on rows of benches awaiting their turn. Lawyers
in well-pressed suits walked about officiously, briefcases in
hand. Suddenly a red-faced bailiff rose: "Hear ye, hear ye,"
shouted the red-faced man. "God bless the United States
and this honorable court." Everyone rose as a tall, black-
robed figure entered and sat down in a gigantic armchair
facing us.

"We are first on the calendar," David whispered, "better
go over what I prepared for you again."

"How long will this take?" I asked.

"Five minutes at the most," said David.

Standing before the judge, I read the litany that David had
prepared for me. Having given hundreds of academic lec-

tures in the past without a single note, I now found myself unable to speak extemporaneously for less than three minutes. I knew that this grim little play I had to act out made me a criminal before the law. Oscar's prophecy was about to come true. I heard myself confessing before the black-robed figure that I had not immediately reported Laura Larrabee's crime to the authorities when I had found out about it and that I had lied to a federal inspector.

"You should have seen a lawyer immediately after John Ashley came to see you," David had said. "Instead, you foolishly protected Laura."

It was true, I thought, I had protected Laura. The thought of reporting her to the authorities had never even occurred to me. After all, we had been lovers. The Via Veneto flashed through my mind. "I want to make you happy," Laura had said. Her eyes had told me that her love was true. They had filled with tears when I had given her the pearl necklace. Perhaps she was a thief, I thought, but a thief who had once loved me.

"I think we were lucky," David said when it was over, "I didn't see any reporters in the room."

"What now?" I asked, following him down the corridor.

"Now comes the difficult part," David said. "In a few weeks, you will be the government's key witness at Laura Larrabee's trial."

"What do I have to do?" I asked.

"It's not so easy," David said. "A young assistant has been assigned to prepare you for the job."

"I hope it isn't Irving Katz," I said.

"No," said David, "his name is Peter Anderson."

"When is her trial?" I asked. Suddenly, my knees had become weak and I had to sit down on a radiator in the courthouse corridor.

"It's only four weeks away," said David. "You'll have a lot of work to do with Anderson." I looked at David, unable to get up from the radiator. "Remember, you are now on the government's side," David said. "You don't have to fear them anymore. But you must tell them the entire truth. They are counting on you for that. If you start to hedge your story and try to protect yourself or Laura, it'll be real trouble. You must tell the truth."

The truth, I thought. What was it really? I knew now that Laura was a crook. What did that make me? Was Oscar right? Would I end up like my father?

My guilty plea fell on the same day as the publication of my book on Henry Kissinger. When I came home, an affectionate letter from Henry was waiting for me on my desk. "When you sell the book to Paramount," Henry had written, "I suggest Robert Redford as the leading man." Henry's humor touched me and I had to smile. And then, suddenly, the total impact of this terrible day hit me. A scream like that of a tormented animal tore itself out of my chest. The scream, to my amazement, seemed to have a life of its own. I was unable to stop. Caroline hit me in the face, her own face white with terror. Gradually, the scream became a wail and finally subsided to a whimper. My wife and I looked at each other without a word.

Peter Anderson, the young assistant assigned the job of coaching me as witness for the prosecution, had an open boyish face and a mass of soft brown hair that had a way of falling down over his forehead. His eyes were clear and warm and would often twinkle with a gentle humor when I stumbled over a particularly embarrassing episode in my affair with Laura. Despite the fact that he too was very young—not yet thirty—he had a sense of empathy and nuance that made him the very opposite of the constipated Katz.

"Remember," Anderson said at the beginning, "just tell the truth and don't worry where the chips may fall."

When, in my eagerness to please him, I tried to anticipate

a question or went off on an irrelevant tangent, he would tactfully bring me back to the main line of the story. "You are not giving a lecture now, Professor," he would say with a gentle laugh, drawing on his pipe. "Just try to be dumb and answer my questions."

It took us more than two weeks of intensive work to prepare for the direct examination. Question after question, then a refinement of each question. When we were informed that the trial had been postponed for two weeks, our pace became a bit more leisurely. We would go to lunch together and talk about things other than my relationship with Laura Larrabee. I had given Anderson a copy of my book on Kissinger, which he read with genuine interest and pleasure. "Another good review, Professor," he would say when I walked into his office in the morning.

Things were not quite so pleasant when Anderson began his effort to prepare me for the cross-examination. Playing the role of Laura's defense attorney, he would bombard me with often brutal questions that were designed to puncture my story and to reduce me to a state of Jellolike confusion. On these occasions, his voice became staccato and I sensed that this young man, with all his gentleness, also had a core of iron. At the end of such a session, Anderson would break into a smile. "Put your feet up, Professor," he would say, "you held up very well today."

During the weeks of our work together, I discovered that Laura was a criminal of international proportions. From the glimpses that Anderson let me have into the case, it appeared that I was only one of many people who had been deceived by her. I saw, not without a certain morbid satisfaction, that some of her unsuspecting victims had not been academics, but sophisticated businessmen, bankers, and industrialists. Apparently, she had used her considerable knowledge and intelligence to orchestrate gigantic schemes of grand larceny that she disguised as projects of international finance. My letters were to give her a measure of credibility.

She had shown them, without my knowledge or permission, to John Ashley and to the North Dakota bank as well as to numerous other potential victims. The eighty thousand dollars she had advanced me for the book project would have been a relatively modest sum, I realized, if as a result of my connections she could have cheated the government of Congo, Brazzaville, out of a million dollars in commissions. It turned out, of course, that the book project was pure invention. Laura had never even met the president of RCA and had paid Mr. Hewitt a sum of money to help her lull my growing fears. I even found a cancelled check made out to him in one of the monthly statements of my account over which Laura had power of attorney. These discoveries were shattering. "I wonder whether she ever really cared for me," I thought out loud on one occasion, more to myself than to Peter Anderson, who was sitting opposite me at his desk. "You might never know, professor," said the prosecutor, drawing on his pipe. "And then again, you might find out at the trial. We'll have to wait and see."

Anderson, I sensed, not only believed my story, but also had begun to like me. A spontaneity had developed between us that came dangerously close to friendship. Then we recalled that he was the prosecutor and I was the defendant who had pleaded guilty to a crime. Both of us were soldiers with a job to do, and yet, there in the bowels of the bureaucracy of the United States Attorney's office, we had encountered one another simply as two human beings. "I know you are not a criminal," Anderson told me after a particularly gruelling session, "but you sure were dumb."

"I have been to see the top people in the criminal division," David said. "There is a chance that they might drop the charge against you." I looked at David, my relief not registering immediately.

During my preparation for the trial, David had been hard at work himself, trying to convince Anderson's and Katz's superiors that, although I might be guilty of misprision, the government should look at my academic contributions, my personal life, and my shattered mental condition, and voluntarily drop the charges. It had been an impossible job, but his persistence had finally borne some fruit. Perhaps, perhaps, I thought to myself.

I had been in hell so long that it had become difficult to face the sunlight.

"It would have been easy for them to say no," David said, "but they didn't. They said they wanted to think it over." I nodded gratefully. The ice around my heart had begun to melt. "Keep up the good work with Anderson," David said. "I think you have an excellent chance."

The trial was postponed a second time. "Every day without a negative decision increases our chances," David said. I began to hope again. Nothing had been reported in the newspapers about my guilty plea. If the charge was dropped, my slate would be wiped clean. My classes were going well. The reviews of the Kissinger book were coming in and were generally favorable. David's hopefulness had given me new strength and my terror had subsided. The weeks went by quickly. But then, one day, just before Thanksgiving, Anderson looked at me gravely.

"Better cancel your class next Monday," he said, "you are the government's first witness."

That evening, I went to see my doctor. Dr. Blaustein, concerned about my fragile equilibrium, had given me some extra sessions. In the middle of the hour, the telephone rang. Dr. Blaustein picked up the receiver.

"Is there nothing more that you can do?" he asked. He listened for a moment and then turned to me. "They have turned you down," he said. "I'm truly sorry."

I grabbed the telephone away from him.

"They made up their minds today: They have decided not to drop the charge," said David.

"After they raised my hopes for two months," I screamed, "they *now* say no?"

"Yes, that's right," said David. "I tried everything," he added.

"What about Anderson?" I shrieked. "He knows what I'm really like."

"Anderson has nothing to do with the decision," David said. "They decided you were guilty of misprision and they will hold you to it."

"There is another item of bad news," Dr. Blaustein said after David had hung up. "David asked me to tell you. There will be an article about you in tomorrow's *New York Times*."

"But I thought there would be no publicity," I said hopelessly, rising from my chair.

"I am truly sorry," Dr. Blaustein said as I walked slowly out the door.

I was waiting at the newsstand as the truck unloaded the next day's *Times*. Only in New York, I thought, do people throw away tomorrow's newspaper. The article was prominent, and was decorated with my picture. None of the eight books I had written, I thought bitterly, had been reviewed with such extraordinary prominence.

I walked toward the Hudson River. It was bitter cold. I wonder whether I will freeze before I drown, I thought with curiosity. It was as if I was thinking about another person. I found myself hoping that it would happen fast. The thought of swallowing all that polluted water seemed repulsive. I had confidence in my heavy winter coat to take me down.

I was in the middle of writing my obituary when I felt a rough jab in my side. Turning my head, I faced a pair of eyes filled with greed and hate.

"Your money, motherfucker," said the man, pointing a knife at me.

Suddenly an electric switch went on inside me. I felt a rage that was so towering that I thought my brain would burst. Oblivious to everything, I lunged at the man with the roar of a wounded lion and hit him with my fists. The mugger dropped the knife and ran. Roaring like a jungle beast, I ran after him, but, slowed down by my heavy winter coat, I finally stopped. Panting clouds of steam into the frozen air, I walked down to the river. But I did not jump. Instead, I screamed my rage and pain across the darkness of the river. Louder and louder I screamed until I felt the liberating tears. And then I understood that this unknown mugger had probably saved my life. As I walked slowly back toward my home, I knew that if I ever took my life, my suicide would be triggered by such an insane helpless rage that it would in fact be murder.

Chapter Twelve

I was sitting in the witness room waiting to be summoned to the stand. The jury had been selected and the prosecution and defense had made their opening statements.

"Just tell the truth," Anderson had said to me before he disappeared into the courtroom.

I had not seen Laura for more than three years. I had been told that she was married now to an extremely wealthy Arab. Within a few minutes, I would have to face her in open court and testify against her. To my amazement, I was completely calm. My brush with death the night before had left me emotionally spent.

The door opened and a clerk motioned me to follow him. He opened a heavy side door for me and pointed in the direction of the witness box. I climbed up a few steps, sat down, looked around, and froze. Directly in front of me, in the defendant's chair, sat Laura, flanked by two attorneys.

I hardly recognized her. She had become so fat that she looked gross. Her hair was bleached to a light blond color which highlighted a general appearance of vulgarity. In front of her was a yellow legal pad on which she was scribbling furiously. She looked up briefly as I took my seat and then bent again over her pad. There had been no sign of recognition. Suspended on her breast I noticed a large and ornate silver cross.

To my right in the judge's chair sat an elderly gentleman with a courtly, rather stern demeanor. The jury, I noticed, consisted of nine women and three men. That's not too good for Laura, I thought without emotion. Women, Harold had once told me, were believed to be harder on other women than were men. In the back were seated a large number of spectators, some with pens poised over pads of paper. Reporters, probably, it crossed my mind. Again, to my surprise, I felt no fear. I rose as a court officer administered the oath. Then I saw Peter Anderson rise from the prosecutor's chair and step up to a little lectern. "What is your name?" he began.

For the next six hours Anderson asked me questions and I answered. When in the course of his interrogation Anderson asked me to define my relationship with Laura, and I described it as a love affair, several of the spectators in the back perked up visibly and the reporters began to scribble on their pads. Laura sat impassively throughout the whole proceedings, looking straight ahead. Once in a while she would write something on her pad and hand it to her lawyer, a dapper-looking man who had a habit of pushing his glasses from his eyes up to his forehead. He objected frequently, but was generally overruled by the judge who seemed to be eager for me to get on with my story. By day's end, I had told most of my melancholy tale. Anderson came into the witness room.

"You are an excellent witness, professor," he said with genuine admiration in his voice. David walked me down the courthouse steps. "You were superb," he said. "After the trial I will try again to get the charge dropped." I looked at David. We had become fond of one another and I knew that he felt guilty for having raised my hopes before.

"Thank you, David," I said, waving to a cab, "I hope I do as well tomorrow under cross-examination."

I was scheduled to give a speech that evening in a small church in a suburb of New Jersey. At the bus terminal, I bought several evening papers. The trial was featured in every one of them in lurid detail. "Sex and Fraud at the UN," one headline said; "Adulterous Love Among the Diplomats," trumpeted another. I read the stories on the bus out to New Jersey, eating a candy bar. I read entirely without emotion. This was happening to someone else, I thought, not me.

The minister was waiting for me on the church steps. His face was grim and his lips were pressed together tightly.

"I tried to call you," he said coldly, "the lecture has been cancelled."

"Why?" I asked calmly. I was curious as to what he would say.

"I think you know the answer to that question," said the minister.

"No, I don't," I said perversely. The man reminded me of the college president who had expelled me more than a quarter of a century ago.

"I do not want confessed adulterers teaching in my church," said the minister with a cold fury in his voice.

"I see that you are improving on your Lord," I managed to retort, "you have decided to cast the first stone."

I took the next bus back to New York City. In a drugstore in the terminal I purchased a bottle of sleeping pills. I knew that I would have to buy them gradually and in different places in order to avoid suspicion. Suicide, it occurred to me, had to be mapped out like a military surprise attack to be successful. Careful and detailed planning was essential. One mistake could botch the job.

Caroline was waiting up for me. She was smiling, but her face betrayed her worry.

"The phone has been ringing all night," she said, trying to keep her voice under control. "Your mother called and said she wished she had died before this happened."

"My God," I said.

"A lot of people have been calling to cancel your lectures," Caroline continued, "and there has been a lot of mail."

I went to my desk and opened some of the envelopes. They were mostly cancellations, hate mail from anonymous moralists, and bills. There were also two letters of encouragement from former students.

"Do we have any plans for tomorrow night?" I asked Caroline.

"No," replied my wife.

"Thank God," I said quietly, "just family." Then, after hiding the sleeping pills in my desk drawer, I turned on the television set. In the middle of the news, I went to sleep.

"This is not a police court," said the judge to Laura's defense attorney. "I wish you would stop these unpleasant mannerisms: Please stop shouting at the witness." The dapper-looking man had been cross-examining me for well over four hours and had been unable to confuse me. In his frustration, he had begun to raise his voice and shake his finger. His questions had become more and more irrelevant and Anderson was rising every two minutes to object. The two men had begun to resemble a couple of jacks-in-the-box alternately rising up in front of me. The judge was watching the proceedings like a bored referee at a tennis match. Clearly, he believed the quality of the match to be inferior and was eager for it to come to a speedy end.

"The witness is being evasive," the defense attorney shouted for the tenth time after I had given an answer that did not suit his purposes.

Finally, the judge lost patience: "The witness seems to be telling the truth whether it hurts him or not," he retorted sharply. Gratefully, I looked at the old man on my right, who had exercised what I thought was justice.

Laura's lawyer tried to make a case that his client had merely overextended herself financially and had never intended to defraud anyone. My testimony to the effect that Laura had disappeared without a trace and had left me in the lurch with Ashley was, of course, devastating to his case. On rebuttal, under questioning by Anderson, I produced the evidence about Laura's attempted fraud in Brazzaville; the shock on Laura's lawyer's face showed visibly. Putting his glasses back on his forehead, he rapidly consulted with his client, who had sat impassively during the entire cross-examination.

"I move to exclude this entire material on grounds of irrelevance," he said.

"Overruled," replied the judge.

"You did well," Anderson said again, shaking my hand. David took me aside. "I think even Katz may have changed his mind about you," he said. "He no longer thinks that you wrote those letters with any intention to defraud."

"Then why doesn't he drop the charge?" I asked.

"I told you I will try after the trial is over," David said.

"I'll wait that long," I said calmly.

Once I was back on the witness stand, Laura's attorney asked me, "To what crime did you plead guilty?"

"Misprision," I replied. "I did not report Laura's crime."

"You are facing ruination, Doctor," said the dapper lawyer. "Why did you plead guilty to a crime when no crime was in fact committed?"

He had taken off his glasses and stared at me expectantly. Immediately, I sensed the trap. With all my heart, I wanted to agree with him. Yes, I yearned to shout, I am not a criminal! But I also knew that if I now repudiated my guilty plea in open court, this would embarrass and infuriate the prosecution, and would make matters worse for me.

"I pleaded guilty freely and voluntarily," I said.

The judge had not addressed me directly during my entire time on the witness stand. At the end of the third day, however, before I was about to be discharged, the old man turned to me and asked: "What are your present feelings toward the defendant, Doctor?" I looked at the courtly little man and suddenly had to think of Laura in Rome five years earlier, smiling at me in the warm Italian sun. The judge looked at me, patiently waiting for my answer. I glanced at the fat woman in front of me. She had stopped scribbling on her pad. Light years stood between us. I turned back toward the judge. His face looked kind and suddenly I lost my composure. I felt the tears streaming down my face. "Would you like a short recess?" the judge asked with genuine concern. I shook my head, unable to stop my tears.

"My heart tells me that she once loved me," I choked out, "but my mind tells me now that she used my connections to make a profit for herself." As I left the stand for the last time, I looked at Laura. I knew that I would never see her again. She was staring back at me, the hate in her eyes bottomless.

"I'll let you know by tonight whether there's a chance they will drop the charge," said David. "Her lawyer didn't lay a glove on you. You couldn't have been a better witness."

"I will be at Dr. Blaustein's, David," I said, thinking of his earlier call. I looked into David's intelligent and open face. "Thank you, David," I said gratefully. "I hope they let me salvage something; I am practically ruined now." Anderson walked up and thanked me warmly. "I guess this is it," I said a bit unsteadily, reaching out to shake his hand. The young prosecutor took it and looked into my eyes. Both of us wanted to say more, but neither of us dared. For the last time, I walked down the courthouse steps.

"I am afraid I have bad news for you," said Dr. Blaustein. He picked up a copy of a national magazine which was lying on his desk. In the crime section, illustrated with a picture of myself and Laura, was a lengthy article entitled "Love and Leverage."

"There are distortions in it," said Dr. Blaustein, "and David is prepared to sue."

"Not a bad title," I said absently. Just then, the phone rang. It was David.

"They have turned you down again," he said.

"What?" I asked. I had heard him all too well.

"They have said no again," David repeated.

"And what about Anderson?" I asked. The entire scene struck me as a rerun of an earlier one.

"Anderson has been taken off the case," said David.

"I'll walk you home," said Dr. Blaustein.

"No, I won't do anything stupid," I promised Dr. Blaustein at the door. He had insisted on taking me up in the elevator. "I am going for a walk," I said to Caroline, opening my desk drawer. I took out the sleeping pills and slipped them in the pocket of my winter coat.

"Let me come with you," said my wife.

"I'll be right back," I answered. "I just want to get a paper."

It was freezing cold again. I walked along Broadway, looking for a small hotel. I saw a flashing neon sign which spelled Hotel. The "T," I noticed, wasn't flashing.

"Ten bucks a night," said the clerk. "Are you alone?"

I nodded. The clerk handed me a key.

"Two-oh-seven," he said without expression. "Checkout time is noon."

I opened the door to Room 207 and switched on the light. A large cockroach scurried under the bed. I switched off the light again, took the pills out of my pocket and put them on the dresser. The bathroom was filthy. A swarm of cockroaches fled under the bathtub when I turned on the light. But then, to my immense relief, I saw what I was looking for: An inverted waterglass was sitting on a tray near

the washbasin. I turned on the faucet and let the water run
till it was clear and cold. Then I filled the glass, switched
off the bathroom light, and walked back into the other room.
I set the glass down on the night table. The neon sign was
flashing right outside the window, covering the shabby fur-
niture with a reddish glow. I took the pills off the dresser
and put them on the night table. Then I sat down on the bed.

A cockroach appeared from under the bed and marched
steadily past my leg. It would be alive tomorrow, it occurred
to me, when I would be a corpse. Annoyed, I lifted my foot,
aiming to crush the bug that would outlive me. The insect
evaded my threatening foot adroitly and fled under the
dresser. I couldn't help but smile in sympathy. For two
hours I had sat on the edge of the bed preparing to swallow
the pills. Twice I held a dozen or so in my mouth and was
about to wash them down when something stopped me and
I foolishly spat them back into my hand.

Survival. All my life I had been a professional survivor.
I had never been taught how to love, but I certainly had
learned how to survive. I could have died six million times
in Auschwitz or Treblinka, and now I was going to finish
Hitler's job. And Oscar's; and my father's. Theirs would
be the posthumous victory. I looked at the deadly pills in
my hand, wet from my saliva. My whole life had been a
struggle to survive and now I was about to recapitulate my
father's fate. The skull in the corner of the little cemetery
in Vienna had finally pulled me in. Oscar's curse had come
to pass. I would follow my dead father.

Six months ago, I had been a happy and successful man.
My reputation had been good and I had toasted Henry
Kissinger and Hans Morgenthau at the dinner table in my
own home. Now everyone knew about me. My old life was
finished. My affair with Laura had ruined me.

As I sat there, immersed in self-pity, it occurred to me that through my suicide I would revenge myself on everybody. I would achieve victory through ultimate defeat. I would not allow my enemies to do me in. By my act of suicide, I would remain master over my own life and death. Let there be darkness. In one single, crashing act of oblivion, I would find my vindication.

And yet, I couldn't get myself to do it. My hand, with the pills in it, had begun to tremble violently. A poem by Kipling that I had read long ago in China as a boy suddenly flashed through my mind: "If you can meet with triumph and disaster, and treat these two impostors just the same," the English poet had written, "then you will be a man, my son." I certainly wasn't acting like a man by the old poet's standards. Pills in hand, I began to think. It was true, I had been manipulated and used and had been the victim of a terrible injustice. It was also true that I had pleaded guilty to a crime when in fact I had not committed one. Yet, I knew too that I was far from innocent.

Gradually, as I sat on the bed, the answer came to me. What had brought me to this pass was my hunger for the outer trappings, the titles and the merit badges, the pursuit of fame and power. The books that I had written were to give me value where I felt none. The famous people whom I had pursued were to cover me with bits of their reflected glory. The lectures that I had delivered were to reap the adulation of a thousand strangers. And my gambling had been the magic wand that was to protect me from facing my ultimate mortality.

Laura Larrabee, it gradually dawned upon me, had been a mirror of my life. At the time I met her, I had gone about as far as I could go. Mine had been a career well done but not one that was truly great. Middle age had come and the end was nearer now than the beginning. Limits would now pervade my life much more than possibilities. Laura's promises had hit me where I was most vulnerable: the hope that somehow, magically, decline could be arrested and youth's climb resumed. Now this illusion had been shattered. My ordeal was forcing me to separate the trappings from the substance, the wasted motion from the inner value. Long ago, I had become someone I was not. If I now decided to go on living, I might finally discover who I was. I would have to start all over.

And what about my wife and child? With a deep sense of shame, I realized that I was about to inflict unbearable and brutal pain on the only human being in the world who had loved me unconditionally and who had loyally stood by me. And almost worse, I was about to inflict upon my little child what had been done to me. Disgusted with my maudlin self-pity, I flung the pills away from me. In the reddish glow of the broken neon light, I saw them scatter all over the bug-infested room.

The reality was clear. If I took my life in longing for my father, I would never find him. I would only find oblivion. If I killed myself in rage over the people who had wronged me, those people would hardly be affected in their glacial indifference. I, however, would be dead. And the two people whom I would have punished would be the very ones who loved and needed me. Some of my friends might perhaps say in sympathy that my troubled past had finally caught up with me. But I knew better: As an adult, I had a measure of free will and had to take responsibility for my mistakes. Suicide, then, would be the most selfish act of an essentially selfish life, an act of absolute and total moral cowardice.

But how was I to go on living now that all my props were ripped away? I would have to accept life without conditions and I would have to build again. Perhaps old Kipling had been right, I thought, as I left the shabby hotel room. Perhaps, finally, at fifty, I had begun to be a man.

"Checking out?" asked the old night clerk at the desk.

"No," I answered, "checking back in," and handed him a twenty-dollar bill.

I was sitting in a cab between Harold and David. Harold had lost a lot of weight since his heart attack almost half a year before. It was a bitter cold day in January and I was about to be sentenced by a federal judge. None of us knew what would happen. Laura Larrabee had been convicted on seven counts of fraud and had received three years in jail. In my case, as the media had pointed out ad nauseam, the maximum penalty for failure to report a felony was three years in prison or a five-hundred-dollar fine or both. I had little left to lose and was prepared for anything. If I received a term in jail, I was determined to survive that, too.

Anderson and Katz were waiting in the courtroom. Both men nodded cordially. I was surprised to see Peter Anderson since David had told me he had been transferred off the case after the trial. Shortly afterward, the red-faced bailiff announced the arrival of the judge and the tall black-robed figure entered. I noticed a few reporters in the gallery. Everyone rose. The scene struck me as both awesome and a bit theatrical. It was as if a play were about to begin and no one but the black-robed figure knew the ending. David rose and spoke briefly and eloquently on my behalf. Then I got up and asked the judge for an exit visa from the hell in which I had been living for three years. "I could not die," I said, "nor, however, can I live."

Now, it was the prosecution's turn. Irving Katz rose to address the judge. My fate might well depend on what this stiff young man would say. To my surprise, Katz did not say a single unkind word. He praised my testimony at the trial and declared that I had played a decisive role in bringing a major criminal to justice. David looked at me and whispered: "He feels guilty as hell about you now."

"I sure hope so," I retorted.

The moment of truth had finally arrived. The judge looked at me sternly and began to read my sentence.

"You won't know until the end, so hang on to the table," whispered David on my right.

Harold, on my left, looked gaunt, staring straight ahead.

"There is a synonym for misprision," the judge began. "It has achieved a melancholy prominence in recent years. The word is cover-up." That's it, I thought, I have been linked to Watergate. Three years in jail. But the judge had moved on to a philosophical discussion of three different types of crime: violent and venal, nonviolent but venal, and nonviolent and nonvenal. Then he proceeded to define my own.

"Violence played no part in it," he said, "neither did thought of personal gain." I couldn't help but feel that the judge was generous. While I believed that I was not a criminal, I had certainly gone after fame and power.

"I perceive in this case nothing more and nothing less than human frailty," said the judge. The tears sprang to my eyes. This man had also understood that I was not a criminal. "Judging by method and by motive," he continued, "your acts are less rather than more severe. Your awareness of wrongdoing was quick, and your remorse complete." He certainly is generous, I thought. My awareness and remorse were of rather recent vintage, born in a roach-infested room. "I perceive no need for personal punishment greater than that already visited upon you," the judge concluded. "A term of imprisonment is entirely inappropriate."

No jail, I thought with relief, and looked at David. The young lawyer squeezed my hand.

"Wait," he said, "the judge is not yet through."

The black-robed man glanced up from his notes and looked at me.

"Our campuses," he said, "are frequently illuminated by the cold brilliance of scholars. Less frequently the lives of their students are warmed by a teacher's human compassion. I see that factor in this case."

It was true, I thought. I did care for my students. There had been an outpouring of sympathy for me and dozens of my former students had written letters to the judge on my behalf.

"There are minds confined in prison that swing from apathy to frustration to despair," the judge continued. "I am satisfied that useful work can be done among the inmates by a teacher of your gifts." My God, I thought, he will sentence me to teach in jail.

"Accordingly," said the judge, "you are to teach in prison for an average time of two hours a week for eighteen months." I sprang to my feet.

"Your Honor," I said with genuine emotion, "it will be a privilege to serve those less fortunate than myself." The words had come out of me spontaneously. The judge's words had moved me deeply.

The black-robed man smiled just a little. "It is my hope," he said, "that this nightmare is now over and that as a result of this program, good may come to others, so that we may achieve that combination of law and mercy which results in justice, a goal which frequently eludes mankind but for which we must continue to aspire."

"It's over," David said, embracing me.

Harold smiled. "We better make sure," he said, "that Laura is not an inmate in the jail where you will teach." I nodded sadly and thought back to that day, light years ago, when Laura had told me that she wished to be my student.

Peter Anderson came up and shook my hand.

"I hope the day will come," I told him, "when we can be friends."

"I do too," said Anderson, his handsome face breaking into a smile.

Caroline had been sitting in the last row. Now she came up and kissed me.

"I'll teach in jail," I said, wiping away my tears.

"That's wonderful," said Caroline, "you can turn the jail into a college."

"I can't wait," I said sincerely. "All my life I have gone after upward mobility, now I'll try it downward; it's probably much more interesting and creative."

My wife looked at me and smiled. She knew I had meant what I had told the judge.

"You are a great teacher," she said, and took my arm. "The prisoners are lucky."

"So am I," I said, kissing her tears away, "believe me, so am I."

As I walked out into the wintry January sun, I was aware of the true nature of my offense. The ancient Greeks had called it *hubris*: presumptuous ambition. Ironically, most of my writings about world politics had dealt with this pervasive theme. Time and time again, nations throughout history had overreached themselves. Some, like Hitler's Germany or Imperial Japan, had to be destroyed completely. Others, like the United States, had to learn and grow through dreadful suffering. Even the leaders of the world's greatest democratic nation would not change their course in Vietnam until they were shaken and shattered into doing so. Nations, like men, seemed to learn primarily through trauma and catastrophe.

I, too, had overreached myself. I had used my intelligence not to question the reckless path on which I had embarked, but to rationalize my acts. And now the gods' rough justice had been meted out. But I had been fortunate. Nations bent on self-destruction seldom had a second chance. Their course toward oblivion usually proved irreversible. This was the challenge of history and its tragedy. It was the shape "destiny" assumed on earth. But if I gave up my illusions and my hubris, I could still stop the engine of destruction.

I resolved to grasp the opportunity to rebuild my life. Within a week, I had worked out a plan whereby twice a week I would offer a college course in world politics to a group of federal prisoners. Those who passed a final examination would earn regular college credit. This opportunity, I thought, might give the prisoners new hope and self-esteem. My plan was approved by the university, and shortly afterward it was endorsed by the warden of a federal penitentiary not far from New York City. An innovative and exciting way to use my teaching talent had suddenly opened up. I sensed that this new prison course might soon develop into a lasting professional commitment.

The myth of Eden records the painful fact that each person must leave his garden of illusion in order to become fully human. The overtones of woe with which this myth has echoed down the ages testify to the reluctance and the pain with which wisdom—and hence full humanity—is born. Perhaps my new assignment would be the beginning of such wisdom.

Chapter Thirteen

There had been an escape from the prison a week before and the guards were nervous. The fugitive had used one of the bathrooms to change from his prison denims into street clothes that his girlfriend had brought during a visit. Then he had simply walked out of the building with the rest of the visitors. Since then the guards counted the five hundred inmates four times every day. The count was late again tonight and I had already been kept waiting in the prison lobby for almost a full hour. My patience was beginning to wear thin.

At last a guard appeared and motioned me to follow him. The walk to the prison classroom was a long and tedious one since we had to traverse a number of empty cells, all of which had to be unlocked and then locked again. My escort was overweight and in no particular hurry as he slammed the cell doors shut, testing each lock carefully.

"Big night tonight, eh?" he asked.

"That's right," I answered. I had been teaching the college course in world politics to a group of prisoners during the past year and this was the night of their final examination. The members of the class had been selected by the warden and I had donated the books.

"Think they'll make it?" asked the turnkey. I noticed a trace of irritation in his voice. "I never got to go to college," he continued. "But nowadays the crooks go to jail and get themselves a college education."

We had reached the classroom and the guard locked the door behind me. I was alone with my students in a federal penitentiary. During the first few weeks it had made me slightly edgy to be locked up with a group of criminals even though a guard was usually posted outside the classroom. Over the months, however, my fear had vanished. I had grown to like my new students and sensed that they appreciated what I had to offer. Gradually, I became involved and began to look forward eagerly to my two evenings a week in jail. Frequently, I stayed on after class and talked to the inmates individually. Now that a year had passed, I had come to know them well and to care for some of them quite deeply. I looked over the class. All nine were there. At the beginning, there had been twenty, but eleven had been transferred to other penal institutions during the year, almost always without warning. When I complained about this practice to a prison official on one occasion, he looked at me with a thin smile and said, "It may be your course, Professor, but it's our jail." There was no malice in his voice, only the indifference of an overburdened bureaucrat.

One of my students, a fifty-five-year-old man who had already served fifteen years of a life sentence, passed out the examination booklets.

"Looks tough," said Claire, looking over the questions. I knew that she was joking. Claire was the extremely pretty twenty-six-year-old daughter of a college professor from Colorado. She already had two degrees and was the best student in the class. Two years before, Claire had fallen in love with a Polish nationalist while studying in Vienna, and had married him after a brief courtship. The Pole had agitated for years against the Communist government that was ruling his homeland, but no one in power had paid the slightest attention to him. Finally, in a fit of frenzy, the young man had hijacked a passenger plane and forced the pilot to fly it halfway around the world in order to attract attention to his cause. He had informed his wife a few days before the hijacking and she had desperately tried to dissuade him, but to no avail. At the last moment, fearing for her husband's life, Claire went along with him and passed out leaflets among the passengers. The thought of reporting the man she loved to the authorities had never even occurred to her. When the plane ran out of fuel and landed in London, the couple surrendered and was promptly extradited to the United States. A jury found the young Pole and his wife guilty of air piracy resulting in a death. As it turned out, the Pole had left a bomb behind in a railroad station locker and a police officer was killed while attempting to dismantle the explosive. Claire had maintained at her trial that she had not known about the bomb, but the jury had not believed her story.

I remembered my conversations with Harold about going to trial in my own case and that he had counseled against it. I began to understand with sadness that there was a great deal more to our criminal-justice system than met the eye, and that law and justice were not necessarily the same.

Both Claire and her husband were given mandatory life sentences, and were shortly to be shipped to different prisons. Claire still loved her husband and her one request to me had been that he be permitted to attend the commencement ceremony that I had arranged for those students who would pass the course.

She had only just begun to grasp the enormity of her predicament.

"My God," she had gasped when she was told of her husband's imminent transfer, "they will destroy my marriage. I will never have children; I'll be an old woman when I get out!"

I was unable to disagree, hence I kept silent. But the

thought that a vibrant young woman who had made one tragic, terrible mistake should be buried alive made me feel sick. When I had suggested to a prison official that justice would be better served if Claire were allowed to hold a regular job under psychiatric supervision, but donated most of her income for twenty years to the dead policeman's family, the man had merely laughed.

"I don't think the American people would stand for that," he had said.

"Would the American people prefer to pay a quarter of a million dollars for her twenty-year incarceration?" I had asked.

"I think so," the official had replied.

Now, as I looked at Claire, I felt impotent and guilty.

"It's the same exam I gave my students at the university," I said. Claire nodded.

Shortly after her conviction, she had written a thoughtful paper on terrorism, pointing out the fact that some terrorists had become prime ministers of the very states for whose nationhood they had fought. While I had serious doubts about Claire's point that only a thin line divided the terrorist from the patriot, I admired her loyalty to the man she loved. She was a forthright, honest person who had fallen in love with a self-destructive, misguided idealist. Now she employed her entire intelligence to rationalize her husband's deed which had cost another human being's life. Her sanity, no doubt, depended on her ability to maintain this rationalization. She would probably serve her sentence in a spirit of martyrdom for a cause that had meant absolutely nothing to her before the fateful meeting with her desperate lover. Whenever I looked at Claire, the refrain from Edgar Allan Poe's poem *The Raven* crossed my mind: "Nevermore! said the raven, nevermore."

"Good luck, Claire," I said.

Saul was looking nervously around the room. He had forgotten his pen again and now there was no way to get out. Ten locked doors separated him from his ballpoint. I lent him mine and he looked at me gratefully. Saul had been a successful lawyer, but had been disbarred and convicted for having sold swampland in Florida to prospective real estate investors. Even though he had made complete restitution to the victims of the land swindle and had gone into bankruptcy to make amends, the judge had taken a dim view of a lawyer running afoul of the law and had given Saul three years. Saul was doing hard time, as the prison jargon put it. He was a compulsive worker and was terrified of idleness. He assisted the rabbi with sabbath services on Friday nights and the priest with church services on Sunday mornings. During the week, he worked as a clerk in the warehouse and in his spare time he prepared parole applications for other prisoners. At night, he did pushups or scrubbed his cell. He could not face the fact that he was serving time in jail and that the stigma would remain with him after his release.

"Prison," he said to me once, "is a place of dehabilitation, not of rehabilitation. Do you know," he asked me, "what it costs to keep me here a year?" I shook my head. "Fifteen thousand dollars!" Saul shouted. "I am not a violent man," he continued. "Would it not have made more sense to let me work for nothing for the Legal Aid Society for three years instead of locking me up and wasting my skills and your money?"

I found it difficult to disagree with Saul and his concept of service rather than imprisonment. But when I mentioned the idea to a correction officer he, too, dismissed it with a laugh. "That wouldn't be much of a punishment," he said. The economics of Saul's argument made no impression on him. He was just one of many prison officials who expressed a need for revenge and punishment. It also became clear to me that prison was a business and a supplier of a variety of jobs. I wondered, though, as I looked at Saul scribbling furiously on his pad, what would become of him after his release. He would never again be permitted to practice his profession. What would his two children think of him? Would the stigma of disbarment and a prison record seduce him back into another shady deal?

I was interrupted in my thoughts. Charles was rising from his chair. He was a large man with bladder trouble and I knew that he had to go to the bathroom. This had posed a problem on numerous occasions during the year. Despite the fact that there was a bathroom adjacent to the class, the guards had refused to issue me a key. The memory of the quick-change escape artist still haunted them. The only way to obtain the key was to knock at the door and hope that a guard would hear. Charles was lucky. Two soft taps at the door summoned Angelo who promptly opened the bathroom door for Charles. "How's it going?" he whispered. Angelo had sat in on a couple of my sessions, but had found the material too difficult and had quietly withdrawn. Nonetheless, he was never jealous or bitter. He was always pleasant and considerate, and whenever he was on duty I could be sure that the class would not be held up by wasteful and arbitrary delays.

Not all the guards were as courteous as Angelo. One particularly nasty type had kept me waiting once in the prison lobby for two hours only to tell me finally with thinly disguised relish that he wouldn't let me in at all. My protest that this was my regular teaching night had only offended his authority. "This is not the street," he said. "I'll give you one minute to get out. Now git!" I left without another word. A letter of complaint that I wrote to the warden afterward got no response.

Charles, visibly relieved, emerged from the bathroom and lumbered back toward his seat. He was serving a one-year sentence for stock fraud. He and Saul were friends although Saul resented the fact that Charles had drawn a lighter sentence for a comparable crime. The subject of different sentences for similar crimes was an unending topic of conversation between the two men. Charles was desperately ashamed of being in jail and had forbidden his wife to visit him. His friends and associates had been told that he was on an extended business trip. As the date of his release approached, Charles was terrified lest the truth about him become known and ruin him in the community. Unable to face that prospect, he was fast sinking into a depression. Freedom to him was a terrible moment of truth when society might discover that he was a criminal.

Angelo lit up a cigarette as he prepared to leave the classroom. Leroy sniffed the air and made a pleading gesture toward Angelo. The guard walked over and handed the prisoner his half-empty pack. Leroy was a bank robber who had already served nine years of a twenty-year sentence. He had taken the course in order to have a better chance when he went before the parole board within the coming year. He had a wife and ten-year-old daughter who lived in a tenement in Harlem. It had taken Leroy half a year to open up to me a little.

"Do you ever see your wife?" I asked him once.

"Yeah, but we are not allowed to be alone," Leroy answered bitterly. "Sometimes I wish the bastards had castrated me," he continued vehemently. "I am only thirty."

Leroy had escaped five years ago and the police had found him the next day at home in bed with his wife. Three more years were added to his sentence. Since then Leroy's rage knew no bounds. But he understood that he had to sit on constant guard duty on his emotions. He had to resist the urge to take offense, to escape, to revolt, or to fight back because another mistake would simply subtract what he had already put behind him and start the wheel rolling again from the beginning. "You can't fight 'em," he said in a heavy voice.

He counted time from one Christmas to another because he was allowed to spend that day with his wife and daughter.

Leroy yearned to make love to his young wife and worried about other men.

"They won't let a man be with his wife but they don't care about homosexuality in jail," he said.

Time to him was like a meter, adding the years, implacably. He had done well in my course and had overcome serious deficiencies in basic education. His entire life was fixated on the obligatory ten-minute interview with the parole board, now only another year away.

"I've got to pass this course, Doc," he said to me almost every week.

I had no doubt that he would. His fellow students told me that Leroy was no longer available for cards or Ping-Pong after work. He studied in his cell at least three hours every night.

I looked at my watch. Almost half of the time allotted for the examination had already passed. The classroom was completely silent. My eye fell on Smoky who was noiselessly cleaning out his pipe. It was almost always in his mouth but I had never actually seen him smoke. Smoky was a lifer who was somewhat of a mystery. He had done fifteen years in different penal institutions and had been transferred a year ago to the prison where I taught my course. A man of considerable intellect and erudition, he chose not to speak about himself, nor did I find it appropriate to question him. Our conversations remained limited to abstract topics, usually philosophical in nature. Smoky's favorite subject was the complex nature of justice. He found it inexhaustible. Once, after a particularly lively dialogue, however, Smoky did let down his reserve.

"Doc," he said, reaching for my hand, "I wish I could do something for you, too."

I was so surprised that I couldn't think of anything to say. I simply shook his hand without a word.

The prison rumor had it that fifteen years earlier, Smoky

had been involved in a violent crime, but no one seemed to be familiar with the specific circumstances of the case. Now Smoky seemed much older than his fifty-five years. I saw no trace of the violence that had been responsible for the ruination of his life. His health was failing and his complexion had a waxen and unhealthy look. Twice during the past hour he had shuffled over to the water cooler for a drink. He was about to rise for yet another trip but didn't seem to have the strength. Quickly, I filled a paper cup with water and took it over to his seat. "Thanks, Doc," Smoky whispered gratefully. "I don't know what's the matter with me tonight."

A wave of sympathy for the aging man came over me as I walked back to my chair. Why had I permitted myself to become so involved? I asked myself for the one hundredth time. After all, none of my students in this class was innocent. I could not come up with a simple answer. The rebel in me was appalled by the indifference and arbitrariness of the prison authorities. There seemed to be little if any emphasis on rehabilitation. Most individual expression was crushed by a relentless, impersonal bureaucracy. It was also true, however, that the students were appreciative and considerate. Every time I appeared, the blackboard was scrubbed clean and one of the inmates handed me a piece of chalk. "We've been waiting for you all week," he said sincerely. I sensed that many of these men and women had not experienced kindness or respect in many years and had learned to bury their emotions well. But when they felt that someone took a genuine interest, their need for warmth quickly broke down their defenses. After half a year, I had found my prison teaching to be so meaningful that I was prepared to make it a permanent commitment. I knew that had I been less fortunate, I, too, might have wound up here. In fact, every time I left the jail, late at night, I felt a pang of guilt. A less empathic or understanding judge could have ruined my life without redemption. But the opportunity to teach in prison, to use my talent rather than rot in jail, had given a new meaning to my life. Dimly, I perceived that my selfish striving for success had somehow always left me empty. I never felt this emptiness when I met my prison class. My human values had undergone a transformation.

I looked over at Smoky. He seemed to have recovered and was absorbed again in the examination. In one of our many conversations, Smoky had maintained that no man was really competent to judge another. He found the inequity in sentencing procedures among different judges appalling and capricious. My reply that greater uniformity in sentencing probably was in the offing left Smoky totally unsatisfied.

"Doc," he said with emphasis, "society must learn to differentiate between the offense and the offender."

"But what about equality before the law?" I managed to retort.

"After all these years," Smoky answered thoughtfully, "I have finally come up with a definition of a criminal."

"And what is that?" I asked, intensely curious.

"A criminal," Smoky said after a lengthy pause, "is someone who destroys himself."

I was so perplexed by this definition that, for a long time, I said nothing. It soon occurred to me, however, that there was a profound logic in Smoky's answer. Each of the prisoners in my class had engaged in a self-destructive act that had landed him in jail. Yet I knew many people who were free outside whom I would consider morally inferior to many of my prison students. But those people had simply not been caught. They had refused to self-destruct. No wonder that I had often sensed with some surprise that the moral quality of prison inmates did not seem to differ very sharply from that of the society that put them there. Smoky's definition of a criminal would probably not appear in any text on criminology, but I thought he had a point.

I was jarred out of my thoughts by a jangling of keys

outside the classroom. The door opened abruptly and a strident voice barked, "Everett!" It was Miss Powell, a particularly aggressive woman guard who apparently took pleasure in yanking prisoners out of my class in order to assert her authority.

"Miss Powell," I said quietly, barely able to conceal my anger, "Tim Everett is taking a final examination." Miss Powell looked at me with a blank stare.

"Orders from the lieutenant," she snapped, "some lights need fixing." I decided not to protest any further. If I provoked her, Miss Powell would probably throw me out. Tim Everett followed her obediently out the door.

"Please try to bring him back as soon as possible," I asked, but Miss Powell simply locked the door without another word.

Tim Everett was an English engineer who loved the sea. He was also a hashish smuggler who regarded his trade not only as a lucrative source of income but also as a form of high adventure. His sloop had outrun the United States Coast Guard and a faster ship had chased him all the way down to Bermuda, where he was finally taken into custody. The United States had demanded extradition and the British had complied. Tim had been in jail a year and was known as Mr. Fixit among the prison staff. A first-class engineer, he was able to repair almost any mechanical malfunction. If anything went wrong in the metal entrails of the prison apparatus, Tim would quickly make a diagnosis and prescribe the proper cure. In his spare time, he liked to listen to classical music. Rumor had it that he had attended the Royal Naval College, at Dartmouth. A self-contained man, he spoke most sparingly.

"What will you do when you get out?" I asked him once.

"I'll go back to the sea," said Tim without a moment's hesitation. Something told me not to pursue the subject further. I suspected that Tim would quickly resume his favorite trade.

Rachel, who had been sitting next to Tim, had a pained expression on her face. Like Tim, she did not speak much and I knew very little about her. She was in prison on a charge of contempt for refusing to testify against her lover, who was in the narcotics importing business. Rachel was good-looking in a slightly vulgar way and one could easily imagine her in a long mink coat rather than her orange prison suit. Whenever I brought food into the prison to be shared by my students after class, she usually helped herself to the largest portion. On one occasion, I had brought in a quiche Lorraine. Rachel sniffed at it and then recoiled in horror.

"It's got ham in it," she said. "I can't eat it. I am Jewish."

In the end, however, unable to resist, she had helped herself to a large slice which she munched without a trace of guilt.

"I'll tell you a story," she said, laughing at my puzzled look, "why I ate the ham. An old rabbi on his deathbed," Rachel began, "asks his son for a ham sandwich. The son is horrified. 'You have lived a holy life,' he berates his father, 'why do you wish to end it with a sin?' 'On the day of judgment,' the old man answers, 'there will be a prosecuting angel and a defending angel. As you know, the prosecuting angel always wins. Then I'll be lashed for my sins and the angel will tell me which sin each stroke is for. It will hurt a lot and I will pray for the end of the beating to come. And then, when I hear the angel say, "and this is for the ham sandwich," I'll know it's over.'"

Rachel laughed and took the last slice of quiche off the paper plate. "It'll be over for me soon," she said. "I should be out of here in a few weeks."

Rachel hoped to join her lover who had fled the country, but whose exact whereabouts were unknown. In class, she showed intelligence and humor, but seldom expressed opinions. She would do well on the examination, I was sure, but I realized that I had no idea who she really was.

Reggie, I had noticed, had not been writing for almost half an hour. Instead, he was sitting in his chair, head in hand, looking puzzled. Apparently, he had difficulty with one of the questions. I walked over to his seat and placed my hand on his shoulder. Reggie looked up at me, despair written on his face.

"Taps for me," he whispered, "it's too tough."

"No, it's not," I countered. "I want you to keep on writing."

"I'll do my best, Prof," Reggie whispered back, "but I think it's way over my head."

Reggie had been a printer and engraver who was doing time for forgery.

"What are you in for?" I had asked him once.

"Selling treasury bills," he answered.

"What's wrong with that?" I questioned.

"Well," said Reggie, "you see, I printed 'em."

Reggie could have gotten fifteen years but he drew a judge who gave him only three. Two years after his arrival in the jail, Reggie made a commitment to give his life to Christ. He learned dental hygiene in the prison and spent eight hours every day cleaning his fellow inmates' teeth. In his spare time, he studied scripture and served as an unofficial welcoming committee for newly arrived prisoners. He had married a pretty Irish girl just before he was incarcerated. His wife visited him as often as the rules allowed and counted the days until his release. The only thing that worried him was whether he would find a job. Society, he felt, was unforgiving toward former criminals. He doubted whether prospective employers would be prepared to take a chance on him. No intellectual, he had nevertheless worked doggedly to pass my course and the "street smarts" that he displayed during discussion periods had often livened up the class. After a lecture on the Vietnam war, he shook his head and sighed, "I never knew that brilliant people could be that dumb. I stole money, but they stole human lives." I

couldn't help but think, listening to Reggie, that all my
degrees and all my books had not protected me against
Laura Larrabee.

There was much discussion in the jail about Reggie's religious conversion. At first, the news was greeted with skep-
ticism, and even laughter. But now, two years later, most of
Reggie's fellow prisoners believed that his new commitment
was entirely authentic. I, too, had a feeling that Reggie was
sincere.

I glanced over at Omus as I walked back to my chair. I
was concerned about him. Omus had come from a broken
home in Harlem and had spent most of his life in jail. His
career of crime had begun with car theft at the age of
seventeen and ten years later he was convicted for armed
robbery and given twenty years. In addition, Omus had a
record for pushing heroin and had himself succumbed to
the addiction. His arms, I had noticed, were full of needle
marks. Nevertheless, Omus had taken remarkable steps toward rehabilitation. He had kicked his habit, had learned
to write English, and earned the equivalent of a high school
diploma. He worked in the kitchen and had learned to cook.
Jail had become a kind of home to him. When the parole
board had turned him down three years ago, he was not
the least upset. The world outside held little promise for
him. In jail, he had a clean cell all to himself, plentiful food,
and even the chance to educate himself. When I asked him
whether he had any family, he shook his head.

"This is my family," he said, pointing to the walls around
him.

"What will you do when you get out?" I asked him once
after he had displayed considerable knowledge about Black
Africa in class.

"Try to get back in," he said.

I wasn't surprised at this reply. After all, eighty percent
of all prisoners who were released sooner or later went back
to jail.

I wondered whether he would pass the exam. His writing skills were only marginal. Yet I was pulling for him since I admired him for his perseverance and his courage.

The two hours were over and I got up to collect the papers.

"Be good to us," said Reggie as he handed me his examination.

I went from chair to chair and gathered up the blue books. Suddenly, a shock went through me. I had looked at Smoky. His face was deathly white and beads of sweat were running down his face.

"Doc," he choked out in a tortured whisper, "it's my heart, I think. Please help me." I ran to the door.

"Guard, guard," I yelled, hammering at the locked door with both my fists. There was no response. "Please!" I screamed. "Please open the door!" Silence still. I turned around. Claire and Rachel had lifted Smoky out of his chair and laid him on the floor. His eyes were glazed over and his breathing came in fits and starts. I took off my coat and placed it under Smoky's head. Then I took his hand in both my own.

"Smoky," I said, "try to breathe quietly. We are getting a doctor." Leroy, pantherlike, leapt to the door and scratched at it with his fingernails.

"Doctor, doctor, get a doctor, a man is dying here!" he screamed, totally beside himself. Rachel bent over Smoky and pressed her mouth to his, trying to pump air into his lungs. Incongruously, I wondered where she had picked up her knowledge of first aid. Smoky's chest heaved and suddenly expanded. A tormented gasp escaped from his throat. We had formed a little circle around him. Only Leroy was still clawing at the door.

Helplessly, I caressed Smoky's hand. And then I saw his eyes open.

"Doc," he said, "I hope I pass the exam."

"Of course you will," I said and gave his hand a squeeze.

I had begun to cry with impotence and pain. Smoky, lying on my coat, turned his head toward me with an effort.

"I mean the big exam, the final one," he whispered, and then he closed his eyes.

When the guard finally came, a lifetime later, Smoky's hand had already grown cold in mine.

Commencement was beautiful and sad. A small room had been set aside for the occasion and the inmates had set up a table and some chairs. The table was covered with a green felt cloth dug up from somewhere by Tim Everett. All of my nine students had passed, but Smoky was already in his grave. The warden did not attend, but had allowed each of my students to invite one family member to the ceremony, including Claire's husband. It was probably the last time the young Pole would see his wife before his transfer to another penitentiary. Claire managed a small smile when she walked up to the table to receive her certificate.

I had not been able to persuade Charles to invite his wife even though he had passed the course with honors. Saul, too, was alone. Leroy, looking proud and angry, was sitting next to his young daughter.

After the ceremony, Rachel prepared a reddish nonalcoholic punch. Homemade chocolate cookies that I had brought for the occasion had been confiscated at the gate because someone had forgotten to fill out a special permission slip for the warden's signature. Reggie beamed with pride as he held hands with his young, attractive wife. Omus came up to me, reaching for my hand. "This is the most important piece of paper in my life," he said, pointing to his diploma. He was scheduled to be shipped to Lewisburg the following morning. Omus's written exam had been borderline at best, but I had given him an oral in the hope that he would pass. I was glad now that he had.

Reggie said a prayer for Smoky and we all bowed our

heads. I hoped we would remember him. All too quickly, the living closed ranks against the dead. Reggie also said something about a jail commencement being a new beginning. I hoped that he was right. Our little group was about to disperse into a most uncertain future. I would miss my first group of prison students. If I had affected them, they, too, had left their mark on me. But I would continue. Soon, I would teach another group of prisoners and yet another. I had found a new vocation.

It was Smoky, though, who had left me the most precious gift. His wish had been prophetic. I had held his hand before he died. At his funeral, I had been wracked by sobs that had erupted without warning from the very center of my being. For a long time, I was unable to stop. Afterward, I felt a quiet sadness that finally gave way to a serenity that I had never known. It became clear to me that I had never had the privilege of mourning. My father had been wrenched out of my life before I fully understood death's meaning. I had blamed myself and the guilt had stayed with me. And so the child was doomed to carry the suicide into manhood. Now, at last, more than four decades later, I stood at my father's burial. Through grieving for Smoky, I also mourned my long-dead father. By permitting me to share his death, a lifer had set me free at last: free to cease being a son and to begin to be a father.